Journey through the Psalms

VOLUME 2
Psalms 73-150

Ron Moore

THE JOURNEY
with Ron Moore

Scripture taken from the Holy Bible, New International Version®, NIV®
Copyright © 1973, 1978, 1984, 2011 by Biblica, Inc.™
Used by permission of Zondervan. All rights reserved worldwide.
WWW.ZONDERVAN.COM
The "NIV" and "New International Version" are trademarks registered in the United States Patent and Trademark Offices by Biblica, Inc.™

Cover design and layout by
Linde Graphics Company, Willoughby, OH 44094

Edited by Heather Tyo and Lori Moore

THE JOURNEY is a registered trademark of
The Journey Ministry, Inc., McMurray, PA 15317

Journey Through The Psalms
Copyright © 2015 by Ronald D. Moore
McMurray, PA 15317
ronmoore.org

ISBN 978-1-4675-9191-1

All rights reserved. No portion of this book may be reproduced in any form without the written permission of the author.

Printed in the United States of America.

JUNE 9

Book III

Psalm 73:1-11

A psalm of Asaph.

Surely God is good to Israel,
    to those who are pure in heart.

But as for me, my feet had almost slipped;
    I had nearly lost my foothold.
For I envied the arrogant
    when I saw the prosperity of the wicked.

They have no struggles;
    their bodies are healthy and strong.
They are free from common human burdens;
    they are not plagued by human ills.
Therefore pride is their necklace;
    they clothe themselves with violence.
From their callous hearts comes iniquity;
    their evil imaginations have no limits.
They scoff, and speak with malice;
    with arrogance they threaten oppression.
Their mouths lay claim to heaven,
    and their tongues take possession of the earth.
Therefore their people turn to them
    and drink up waters in abundance.
They say, "How would God know?
    Does the Most High know anything?"

The Slippery Slope of Envy

OK, I'll admit it. I look around at those I consider arrogant and prideful (yes, that's judgmental) and say, "Come on, God, why do you let those kinds of people prosper?! Some say they are on your side. They promote a watered-down message that elevates them and produces wealth. Call them into account for goodness sakes!"

That is Asaph's complaint in this psalm. As a leader of one of David's choirs he was doing ministry . . . the right way. Then he looked around at the arrogant and their prosperity. They had record deals, book deals, nice homes, vacations, thousands of friends on social media, and all kinds of money. Asaph said, "my feet almost slipped; I had nearly lost my foothold. For I envied the arrogant . . ."

Here's the lesson I learn from these verses: Envy makes me lose my spiritual footing. It makes my heart cynical and calloused. It clouds the focus I need to work on my own heart. Envy wastes my time and energy. Envy spends the precious moments of my life and gives no return on investment.

Father, forgive me. Like Asaph, my feet almost slipped. Lord, redirect my focus to see the things in my life that need attention. Take envy far from my heart. In Jesus' name. Amen.

JUNE 10

Psalm 73:12-20

A psalm of Asaph.

This is what the wicked are like –
    always free of care, they go on amassing wealth.

Surely in vain I have kept my heart pure
    and have washed my hands in innocence.
All day long I have been afflicted,
    and every morning brings new punishments.

If I had spoken out like that,
    I would have betrayed your children.
When I tried to understand all this,
    it troubled me deeply
till I entered the sanctuary of God;
    then I understood their final destiny.

Surely you place them on slippery ground;
    you cast them down to ruin.
How suddenly are they destroyed,
    completely swept away by terrors!
They are like a dream when one awakes;
    when you arise, Lord,
    you will despise them as fantasies.

A Clear View in Worship

In the first eleven verses of Psalm 73, Asaph was irritated. The "wicked" seemed to always be getting ahead. Envy boiled in his heart. He almost lost his spiritual footing. The frustration continued in today's passage.

The wicked, Asaph observed, were going through life free of care, making piles of money. Asaph was doing his best to keep his heart pure, his hands innocent, and his head above water. His efforts, however, were without rewards. All this "troubled [him] deeply" until he went into the "sanctuary of God." Worship helped him gain perspective.

Asaph was reminded that life is short and eternity is long. Every person will stand before God to give an account. On that day God will not be impressed with piles of money.

Father, help us keep our focus on what is truly important. Help us to live today with eternity always in mind. In Jesus' name. Amen.

JUNE 11

Psalm 73:21-28

A psalm of Asaph.

When my heart was grieved
    and my spirit embittered,
I was senseless and ignorant;
    I was a brute beast before you.

Yet I am always with you;
    you hold me by my right hand.
You guide me with your counsel,
    and afterward you will take me into glory.
Whom have I in heaven but you?
    And earth has nothing I desire besides you.
My flesh and my heart may fail,
    but God is the strength of my heart
    and my portion forever.

Those who are far from you will perish;
    you destroy all who are unfaithful to you.
But as for me, it is good to be near God.
    I have made the Sovereign Lord my refuge;
    I will tell of all your deeds.

Presence! Protection! Security! Forever!

Asaph was discouraged. Even though he was the leader of one of King David's three Levitical choirs; even though he was serving the Lord; Asaph "envied the arrogant when [he] saw the prosperity of the wicked." Then he gained an eternal perspective. In contrast to the temporary gains of the "wicked," Asaph noted "The God Advantage." Check out four benefits found in today's passage.

> *I am always with you.* The personal relationship we have with the eternal God is more precious than any earthly possession. The Creator is always with us, living in us. Presence!
>
> *You hold me by my right hand.* Asaph said, ". . . My feet had almost slipped; I had nearly lost my foothold," but the Father held him steady with his strong right hand. Security!
>
> *You guide me with your counsel.* As we approach forks in the road, God warns us of the dangerous path and guides us along the right way. God's Word is light for the journey. Protection!
>
> *And afterward you will take me into glory.* After this short time on earth there awaits an eternity (!) for all who know God through his Son, Jesus Christ – Forever!

Father, thank you that death is only a transition into eternal life. Thank you that one day you will take me into glory where I'm breathing only your air. Thank you that one day I'll see you brighter than I'm used to. Thank you that one day you will take me there! In Jesus' name. Amen.

JUNE 12

Psalm 74:1-11

A maskil of Asaph.

O God, why have you rejected us forever?
    Why does your anger smolder against
    the sheep of your pasture?
Remember the nation you purchased long ago,
    the people of your inheritance, whom you redeemed –
    Mount Zion, where you dwelt.
Turn your steps toward these everlasting ruins,
    all this destruction the enemy has
    brought on the sanctuary.

Your foes roared in the place where you met with us;
    they set up their standards as signs.
They behaved like men wielding axes
    to cut through a thicket of trees.
They smashed all the carved paneling
    with their axes and hatchets.
They burned your sanctuary to the ground;
    they defiled the dwelling place of your Name.
They said in their hearts, "We will crush them completely!"
    They burned every place where God
    was worshiped in the land.

We are given no signs from God;
    no prophets are left,
    and none of us knows how long this will be.
How long will the enemy mock you, God?
    Will the foe revile your name forever?
Why do you hold back your hand, your right hand?
    Take it from the folds of your garment and destroy them.

Reaping

The divided heart of King Solomon led to the division of his kingdom. After his death civil war split the country in two – Israel in the north and Judah in the south. The Assyrians conquered Israel in 722 BC and took the people captive. In 586 BC, Jerusalem fell to the Babylonians. This psalm describes the fall.

God's people turned their backs on him. Again and again he sent prophets to get their attention and to warn them of coming doom, but each time they mocked the messengers of God. Like a loving father disciplines his children, so our loving Father brought the Babylonians into play. They smashed the beautifully carved paneling of the temple and set it on fire. "They burned every place where God was worshiped in the land."

As it was in the land of Israel, so it is in our lives. The solemn truth is this: We will reap what we sow. Sow obedience and reap God's blessing.

Father, remind us often of that solemn truth. Help us to sow the things today that will grow great blessing in our lives tomorrow. In Jesus' name. Amen.

JUNE 13

Psalm 74:12-17

A maskil of Asaph.

But God is my King from long ago;
> he brings salvation on the earth.

It was you who split open the sea by your power;
> you broke the heads of the monster in the waters.

It was you who crushed the heads of Leviathan
> and gave it as food to the creatures of the desert.

It was you who opened up springs and streams;
> you dried up the ever-flowing rivers.

The day is yours, and yours also the night;
> you established the sun and moon.

It was you who set all the boundaries of the earth;
> you made both summer and winter.

Rise Up, O God

In the first part of this psalm (74:1-11), Asaph described the hardship that Israel had experienced and asked, "Why?" Then he took a deep breath and reviewed God's work in the past (74:12-17). That gave him confidence for the present challenges. Now, in this final section, he put his request before God.

Asaph asked God to come to the rescue. He pleaded with God to "Rise up . . . and defend your cause." He prayed that God would not forget his people or his covenant with them. Asaph asked that God would work in such a powerful way that "the poor and needy praise your name."

We never have to be general about our requests, as in "God please bless the world." God desires specifics. Specifics allow him to demonstrate his work in memorable ways. When God delivers there are no coincidences. His divine fingerprints are all over the answers to our prayers.

Father, we know you hear and answer our prayers because you have answered them so many times in the past. Here we are again today, in great need of your touch. Reach down, meet us here and then take us where you want us to be. In Jesus' name. Amen.

JUNE 15

Psalm 75:1-5

For the director of music. To the tune of "Do Not Destroy." A psalm of Asaph. A song.

We praise you, God,
> we praise you, for your Name is near;
> people tell of your wonderful deeds.

You say, "I choose the appointed time;
> it is I who judge with equity.
When the earth and all its people quake,
> it is I who hold its pillars firm.
To the arrogant I say, 'Boast no more,'
> and to the wicked, 'Do not lift up your horns.
Do not lift your horns against heaven;
> do not speak so defiantly.'"

Creator and Sustainer

God is not only the Creator, he is the Sustainer. He is the One who chooses the appointed times. Days, months and years are under his sovereign control. He truly holds the heart of every ruler in his hand. He is the author of history.

God is not only the Creator, he is the Sustainer. When uncertainty shakes the world, he holds the pillars firm. When one country moves against another God is overseeing it all and working every move for his purposes.

God is not only the Creator, he is the Sustainer. Nothing in our lives is outside of his view; no movement is beyond his direction. When our world is shaken, he holds our pillars strong so we can live with unshakeable faith.

Father, my heart is unsettled. Things are hitting from all directions. My life is shaken. Remind me in a vivid way of your sovereign hand behind it all. Steady me. Let me tell others of your wonderful work in my life. Thank you for always being near. In Jesus' name. Amen.

JUNE 16

Psalm 75:6-10

For the director of music. To the tune of "Do Not Destroy." A psalm of Asaph. A song.

No one from the east or the west
>   or from the desert can exalt themselves.
It is God who judges:
>   He brings one down, he exalts another.
In the hand of the Lord is a cup
>   full of foaming wine mixed with spices;
he pours it out, and all the wicked of the earth
>   drink it down to its very dregs.

As for me, I will declare this forever;
>   I will sing praise to the God of Jacob,
who says, "I will cut off the horns of all the wicked,
>   but the horns of the righteous will be lifted up."

Lifted Up!

Do you ever feel like the wicked are getting all the breaks? The one who cuts corners gets ahead? Those who are shady get all the sun? Certainly, there are stretches of time when it seems that those who oppose God are getting ahead, but that is a mirage.

The psalmist reminds us that people cannot "exalt themselves." God may let the wicked rise, but in his timing he will bring them down. They may show off their horns (symbol of power) today, but he will cut off their horns tomorrow. The wicked will not prosper.

It's a different story for those who follow hard after God. Instead of his judgment we receive his continuous grace. Instead of wrath, we are covered with his perfect love. Our power is not cut; it is lifted up, for our power comes directly from him.

Father, thank you for lifting me up today. Thank you for giving me strength and power. Thank you for giving me everything I need to do what you are calling me to do. In Jesus' name. Amen.

JUNE 17

Psalm 76:1-6

For the director of music. With stringed instruments.
A psalm of Asaph. A song.

God is renowned in Judah;
    in Israel his name is great.
His tent is in Salem,
    his dwelling place in Zion.
There he broke the flashing arrows,
    the shields and the swords, the weapons of war.

You are radiant with light,
    more majestic than mountains rich with game.
The valiant lie plundered,
    they sleep their last sleep;
not one of the warriors
    can lift his hands.
At your rebuke, God of Jacob,
    both horse and chariot lie still.

Protection and Provision

It's time to sing a song of victory! It's time to rejoice and be glad that this is the day the Lord has made and given to you. God is at work. He has sustained you and provided for you. The roof over your head and the food you eat are reminders that God is on your side and fighting for you.

Asaph, the writer of this song, proclaimed the greatness of God, who lived among his people and fought for them. The enemies' most powerful weapons of war were no match for the God of Jacob. He broke to pieces flashing arrows, shields and swords. With his word alone, he rendered the horse and chariot ineffective.

So . . . sing a song of victory! There will be more battles tomorrow. More enemies will come with their swagger, but thank God for today. He is at work in your life. He is your constant sustainer and provider. He will always give you everything you need to do what he is calling you to do. You can't miss him. Just look toward the light.

Father, our prayers are too often filled with a list of requests. Today we thank you for who you are and how you work in real life. Thank you for homes that keep us warm. Thank you for your provision of daily nourishment. Keep us looking toward you. May we always be encouraged by your work in our lives. In Jesus' name. Amen.

JUNE 18

Psalm 76:7-12

For the director of music. With stringed instruments.
A psalm of Asaph. A song.

It is you alone who are to be feared.
    Who can stand before you when you are angry?
From heaven you pronounced judgment,
    and the land feared and was quiet –
when you, God, rose up to judge,
    to save all the afflicted of the land.
Surely your wrath against mankind brings you praise,
    and the survivors of your wrath are restrained.

*Make vows to the L*ORD *your God and fulfill them;*
    let all the neighboring lands
    bring gifts to the One to be feared.
He breaks the spirit of rulers;
    he is feared by the kings of the earth.

Promises Made . . . Promises Kept

What promises have you made to God?

Marriage for as long as we both shall live

Parenting according to his Word

Using resources to honor him

Being a light in your office

Standing for him in your school

Integrity in the workplace

Reading his Word daily

A reinvigorated discipline of prayer

Using your gifts to serve others

Sharing the Gospel

When you make promises
to the Lord your God . . . fulfill them.
He is honored – not by lip service.
God is honored by obedience.

Father, remind us often of vows we have made to you. Give us the daily strength to fulfill them. In Jesus' name. Amen.

JUNE 19

Psalm 77:1-9

For the director of music. For Jeduthun.
Of Asaph. A psalm.

I cried out to God for help;
> *I cried out to God to hear me.*
When I was in distress, I sought the Lord;
> *at night I stretched out untiring hands,*
> *and I would not be comforted.*

I remembered you, God, and I groaned;
> *I meditated, and my spirit grew faint.*
You kept my eyes from closing;
> *I was too troubled to speak.*
I thought about the former days,
> *the years of long ago;*
I remembered my songs in the night.
> *My heart meditated and my spirit asked:*

"Will the Lord reject forever?
> *Will he never show his favor again?*
Has his unfailing love vanished forever?
> *Has his promise failed for all time?*
Has God forgotten to be merciful?
> *Has he in anger withheld his compassion?"*

Night Cries

It can get lonely at night. When it's just you and God – waiting for sleep. Sometimes those moments of silence produce songs of praise; sometimes cries of pain. There had been times for songs of praise in the night for Asaph, but this night was not one of them.

Asaph was crying out to God for help. His heart was filled with distress, groaning, fatigue . . . and questions. How long would the pain continue? Were God's favor and love things of the past? Had God forgotten his promises and mercy? Where was God's compassion? Sleep would not come; questions would not stop.

Been there? There now? We learn from this portion of the psalm that it's all right to tell God what's on your mind and ask the questions that fill your thinking. In tomorrow's portion of the psalm, Asaph will reflect on what God has done, but this night is filled with cries and questions . . . and that's OK.

Father, sometimes I just have to get my questions out in the air. Like Asaph, I am crying out, groaning and questioning. Thank you for loving me so much that you will let me express my heart. Thank you for always hearing my pleas. In Jesus' name. Amen.

JUNE 20

Psalm 77:10-15

For the director of music. For Jeduthun.
Of Asaph. A psalm

Then I thought, "To this I will appeal:
> the years when the Most High stretched out his right hand.

I will remember the deeds of the Lord;
> yes, I will remember your miracles of long ago.

I will consider all your works
> and meditate on all your mighty deeds."

Your ways, God, are holy.
> What god is as great as our God?

You are the God who performs miracles;
> you display your power among the peoples.

With your mighty arm you redeemed your people,
> the descendants of Jacob and Joseph.

A Past Tense Prayer

The best predictor of the future is a person's actions of the past. So it is with God. In the first part of this psalm, Asaph recorded his desperate pleas in the night. He was alone and afraid. He felt God had forgotten him. Then he collected his thoughts and focused on God's past work.

In remembering the things that God had done, Asaph's questions turned into statements of facts. God is perfect and his ways are perfect. There is no god as great as our God. God performs miracles and displays his great power. With his mighty arm he delivered his people.

Reviewing what God has done in our past is not a religious spin that makes us feel better about our present situation. Rather, reviewing God's work takes our thoughts off present circumstances and places them on the Person of God with whom we have history. When we think of the times God has worked in our past, we can be confident that he will work in our present.

Father, thank you for giving me evidence that you are at work in my life. Thank you for working in my past (review what God has done in your life to this point). I know, Lord, that you never change. I look forward to seeing how you will work in my present. In Jesus' name. Amen.

JUNE 21

Psalm 77:16-20

**For the director of music. For Jeduthun.
Of Asaph. A psalm**

The waters saw you, God,
*   the waters saw you and writhed;*
*   the very depths were convulsed.*
The clouds poured down water,
*   the heavens resounded with thunder;*
*   your arrows flashed back and forth.*
Your thunder was heard in the whirlwind,
*   your lightning lit up the world;*
*   the earth trembled and quaked.*
Your path led through the sea,
*   your way through the mighty waters,*
*   though your footprints were not seen.*

You led your people like a flock
*   by the hand of Moses and Aaron.*

Leading and Following

Your nights may be dark and your songs may be few, but God is not finished with you! His ways – beyond our understanding – are to give us a future that honors him and displays his power.

Asaph began this psalm with desperate cries. Then he reviewed God's work. The waters of the Red Sea "saw you and writhed." They were opened to allow a people in a desperate situation to find safety on the other side. God opened up a path through the mighty waters and he is still leading his people to places of safety today.

God is not finished with you! He has worked in your past. He is at work in your present. He will be at your side in the future. He will once again come to your rescue. He is the God who saves.

Father, the night is dark. I trust in the Light of the World. I am going under. I trust in the One who saves. My cries are desperate. I trust in the One who hears and answers. I will wait on you to lead me and I look forward to singing songs of praise. In Jesus' name. Amen.

JUNE 22

Psalm 78:1-8

A maskil of Asaph.

My people, hear my teaching;
>> listen to the words of my mouth.
I will open my mouth with a parable;
>> I will utter hidden things, things from of old –
things we have heard and known,
>> things our ancestors have told us.
We will not hide them from their descendants;
>> we will tell the next generation
the praiseworthy deeds of the Lord,
>> his power, and the wonders he has done.
He decreed statutes for Jacob
>> and established the law in Israel,
which he commanded our ancestors
>> to teach their children,
so the next generation would know them,
>> even the children yet to be born,
>> and they in turn would tell their children.
Then they would put their trust in God
>> and would not forget his deeds
>> but would keep his commands.
They would not be like their ancestors –
>> a stubborn and rebellious generation,
whose hearts were not loyal to God,
>> whose spirits were not faithful to him.

Show and Tell Parenting

Remember the elementary school assignment of "Show and Tell"? It was a great time to bring a favorite toy, a cool picture, or even a real live person to show your classmates and tell them about the thing . . . or person. "Show and Tell," however, is not just a childhood exercise.

The tradition of spiritual instruction is to teach our children the essentials of the faith and show them how it works. When we teach our children and they see how it works in real life, they will, in turn, teach their children. Effective teaching today allows us to instruct "even children yet to be born."

Now, here's the trick of parenting by "Show and Tell." What we say will be either confirmed or rejected by what we do. Let's face it – the onus of teaching is on the teacher, not the learner.

Lord Jesus, please help us teach our children well. Help us to not nullify our words by our actions. Help us to teach our children about you. Then help us show them what it looks like to follow hard after you all the days of our lives. In your name. Amen.

JUNE 23

Psalm 78:9-16

A maskil of Asaph.

The men of Ephraim, though armed with bows,
> turned back on the day of battle;
they did not keep God's covenant
> and refused to live by his law.
They forgot what he had done,
> the wonders he had shown them.
He did miracles in the sight of their ancestors
> in the land of Egypt, in the region of Zoan.
He divided the sea and led them through;
> he made the water stand up like a wall.
He guided them with the cloud by day
> and with light from the fire all night.
He split the rocks in the wilderness
> and gave them water as abundant as the seas;
he brought streams out of a rocky crag
> and made water flow down like rivers.

Engaged in the Battle

Satan is not that concerned when we deny God. The results are the same if we simply forget him. We don't have to be an atheist to believe like one. We can have crosses on our necks and fish signs on our cars, but that does not guarantee God's guidance in our lives.

The soldiers of Israel's Northern Kingdom had all the equipment they needed, but when push came to shove they were not willing to use their weapons. They forgot all God had done and turned from the battle. God's instruction for living was pushed aside to follow the path of their choosing.

What about you? Are you engaged in the battle? Are you committed to live by God's instruction regardless of the cost? Are you devoted to remember all that God has done in the past in order to live with confidence in the present? Remember, it is just as dangerous to forget God as it is to deny him.

Father, help me to engage in the battle. Don't let me run from it. Don't let me forget your work in my life. Keep me living by your instruction. Don't let me make up my own guidelines for life. Don't let me forget you. In Jesus' name. Amen.

JUNE 24

Psalm 78:17-22

A maskil of Asaph.

But they continued to sin against him,
  rebelling in the wilderness against the Most High.
They willfully put God to the test
  by demanding the food they craved.
They spoke against God;
  they said, "Can God really
  spread a table in the wilderness?
True, he struck the rock,
  and water gushed out,
  streams flowed abundantly,
but can he also give us bread?
  Can he supply meat for his people?"
When the Lord heard them, he was furious;
  his fire broke out against Jacob,
  and his wrath rose against Israel,
for they did not believe in God
  or trust in his deliverance.

Can God Provide . . . Again?

"Well . . . sure, God came through yesterday, but will he come through again today?" "God provided what we needed last month, but I am not sure he will or can take care of this month." "I know, I know . . . God helped me through the last situation, but I'm panicked about this one."

The people of Israel saw God at work. They witnessed the ten plagues that forced Pharaoh to release them. They crossed the Red Sea on dry ground and watched it close in on the pursuing Egyptian army. They were thirsty and watched as God provided water. They witnessed all that God had done and then said, "OK, not bad; but can he also provide us something to eat?"

God gets tired of our short memory and constant lack of faith. In Romans Paul asked, "If God is for us, who can be against us? He who did not spare his own Son, but gave him up for us all – how will he not also, along with him, graciously give us all things?" (Romans 8:31). God has provided eternity for us! Certainly, he can provide all we need until we get home.

Father, thank you for taking care of my eternity through Jesus. I believe that, but I struggle with having the trust for my day-to-day needs. Forgive me. Remind me. Help me in my lapses of faith. In Jesus' name. Amen.

JUNE 25

Psalm 78:23-31

A maskil of Asaph.

Yet he gave a command to the skies above
>> and opened the doors of the heavens;
he rained down manna for the people to eat,
>> he gave them the grain of heaven.
Human beings ate the bread of angels;
>> he sent them all the food they could eat.
He let loose the east wind from the heavens
>> and by his power made the south wind blow.
He rained meat down on them like dust,
>> birds like sand on the seashore.
He made them come down inside their camp,
>> all around their tents.
They ate till they were gorged –
>> he had given them what they craved.
But before they turned from what they craved,
>> even while the food was still in their mouths,
God's anger rose against them;
>> he put to death the sturdiest among them,
>> cutting down the young men of Israel.

All You Need When You Need It

Psalm 78 is a review of how God provided for Israel throughout their history. He delivered them, sustained them and led them – and sometimes he had to teach them hard lessons.

After God freed them from slavery, opened the Red Sea, took care of the Egyptians, and gave them food and water, some people in Israel started complaining . . . again. They were tired of eating the manna and wanted some meat, so he gave them all the quail they could eat. "They ate till they were gorged – he had given them what they craved." Then he disciplined the ones who had forgotten his goodness and questioned his love.

God reminds us time and again that he will provide. If you are anxious for something to happen in your life, stay confident in God's power to provide. Wait for his perfect timing. You can be sure that he will give you just what you need, just when you need it – every time.

Father, I am tempted to take matters into my own hands. Help me leave them with you. I am tempted to run ahead. Help me follow you. I am tempted to question. Help me trust you. In Jesus' name. Amen.

JUNE 26

Psalm 78:32-39

A maskil of Asaph.

In spite of all this, they kept on sinning;
> in spite of his wonders, they did not believe.

So he ended their days in futility
> and their years in terror.

Whenever God slew them, they would seek him;
> they eagerly turned to him again.

They remembered that God was their Rock,
> that God Most High was their Redeemer.

But then they would flatter him with their mouths,
> lying to him with their tongues;

their hearts were not loyal to him,
> they were not faithful to his covenant.

Yet he was merciful;
> he forgave their iniquities
> and did not destroy them.

Time after time he restrained his anger
> and did not stir up his full wrath.

He remembered that they were but flesh,
> a passing breeze that does not return.

God's Restraint

The people of Israel saw God at work up close and personal, yet they had some serious lapses of faith. Many times after God's discipline they returned to him. They acknowledged him as their Rock and Redeemer. Then they forgot and turned away . . . again. "Their hearts were not loyal to him."

God could have wiped out the whole lot, but he remembered the frailty of the human state and showed mercy. The psalmist wrote, "Time after time he restrained his anger and did not stir up his full wrath." He pardoned all their sins.

We can relate to the Israelites. Too often we take God's goodness for granted and complain when we don't get what we think we deserve. We forget that he is our Rock and our Redeemer. Aren't you thankful for God's grace and mercy?

Father, thank you for remembering that I am "but flesh." Thank you for your love, grace and mercy. You are my Rock and my Redeemer. Help my complaints to be fewer and my praise for you to increase. In Jesus' name. Amen.

JUNE 27

Psalm 78:40-49

A maskil of Asaph.

How often they rebelled against him in the wilderness
      and grieved him in the wasteland!
Again and again they put God to the test;
      they vexed the Holy One of Israel.
They did not remember his power –
      the day he redeemed them from the oppressor,
the day he displayed his signs in Egypt,
      his wonders in the region of Zoan.
He turned their river into blood;
      they could not drink from their streams.
He sent swarms of flies that devoured them,
      and frogs that devastated them.
He gave their crops to the grasshopper,
      their produce to the locust.
He destroyed their vines with hail
      and their sycamore-figs with sleet.
He gave over their cattle to the hail,
      their livestock to bolts of lightning.
He unleashed against them his hot anger,
      his wrath, indignation and hostility –
      a band of destroying angels.

The Danger of Victory

Difficult times often follow great spiritual victory. The prophet Isaiah depended on God to singlehandedly defeat the prophets of Baal, then ran from the wicked Queen Jezebel. Peter's great confession of Jesus was followed by his great denial. David built a powerful kingdom, but then there was that encounter with Bathsheba.

Israel had experienced one of the defining moments of the Old Testament. God miraculously delivered them from slavery in Egypt. However, after the deliverance they spent 40 years wandering in the desert. They forgot about God's power and put him to the test.

Spiritual victories are fantastic. Mountaintop experiences are exhilarating, but be careful coming back down to the foothills. Scripture reminds us that Satan hits us when and where we are most vulnerable. After the triumphs he is there to trip us up.

Father, thank you for the spiritual highs. Thank you for the elation of elevation, but please don't let us drop our guard. Remind us that with spiritual victory often comes vulnerability. In Jesus' name. Amen.

JUNE 28

Psalm 78:50-55

A maskil of Asaph.

He prepared a path for his anger;
    he did not spare them from death
    but gave them over to the plague.
He struck down all the firstborn of Egypt,
    the firstfruits of manhood in the tents of Ham.
But he brought his people out like a flock;
    he led them like sheep through the wilderness.
He guided them safely, so they were unafraid;
    but the sea engulfed their enemies.
And so he brought them to the border of his holy land,
    to the hill country his right hand had taken.
He drove out nations before them
    and allotted their lands to them as an inheritance;
    he settled the tribes of Israel in their homes.

Crazy Turns

Life can take some crazy turns. A small lump changes our schedule to include surgery and treatment. An infection turns a routine procedure into months of antibiotics. Some jobs don't work out. Some relationships don't end well. Some kids don't come back home.

Israel lived under the heavy hand of slavery – until God said, "Enough!" God freed his people by showing Pharaoh his convincing power. Then, like a loving shepherd with his sheep, he "brought his people out like a flock." He guided them safely through dangerous paths. His presence calmed their fears.

The Lord is our shepherd. He leads us through those crazy turns. He promises to never leave nor forsake us. Trust the Shepherd with your journey. He will guide you safely home.

Father, I trust you as the sheep trust their shepherd. Thank you for your presence. Guide me through this rough path in my journey. Let me hear your calming voice. Let me feel your strong embrace. In Jesus' name. Amen.

JUNE 29

Psalm 78:56-64

A maskil of Asaph.

But they put God to the test
> and rebelled against the Most High;
> they did not keep his statutes.

Like their ancestors they were disloyal and faithless,
> as unreliable as a faulty bow.

They angered him with their high places;
> they aroused his jealousy with their idols.

When God heard them, he was furious;
> he rejected Israel completely.

He abandoned the tabernacle of Shiloh,
> the tent he had set up among humans.

He sent the ark of his might into captivity,
> his splendor into the hands of the enemy.

He gave his people over to the sword;
> he was furious with his inheritance.

Fire consumed their young men,
> and their young women had no wedding songs;

their priests were put to the sword,
> and their widows could not weep.

Playing the Grace Card

***Grace:** God gives us what we don't deserve.*
***Mercy:** God doesn't give us what we do deserve.*

Everyone loves grace and mercy. We wouldn't exist without them. God's free gift of salvation is wrapped in grace. God's sustaining work of spiritual growth is undergirded by grace. God's gift of the Holy Spirit is his grace empowered. We love grace and mercy. That's why we have a problem with today's passage.

Along with God's grace and mercy is his hatred of sin. Sin is contrary to his Person and against his instruction. He hates sin so much that he sent Jesus to carry our sins to the cross – and sin has consequences. Whatever a man sows that will he also reap.

We will continue to embrace grace. It really is amazing, but it's not to be used as a trump card to sin. Let's be as adamant about obedience before we sin as we are with grace afterward.

Father, thank you for your amazing grace. May we never take it for granted. May we never use it as a license to sin. Don't let us play the grace card when we desire to wander from your instruction. In Jesus' name. Amen.

JUNE 30

Psalm 78:65-72

A maskil of Asaph.

Then the Lord awoke as from sleep,
> *as a warrior wakes from the stupor of wine.*

He beat back his enemies;
> *he put them to everlasting shame.*

Then he rejected the tents of Joseph,
> *he did not choose the tribe of Ephraim;*

but he chose the tribe of Judah,
> *Mount Zion, which he loved.*

He built his sanctuary like the heights,
> *like the earth that he established forever.*

He chose David his servant
> *and took him from the sheep pens;*

from tending the sheep he brought him
> *to be the shepherd of his people Jacob,*
> *of Israel his inheritance.*

And David shepherded them with integrity of heart;
> *with skillful hands he led them.*

In the Sheep Pens

I believe a burning passion for God is kindled in the midst of the normal everyday "sheep pens" of life – carpooling kids to practice; making house payments; repairing leaky toilets; contemplating career changes; building a marriage; working through conflict; and paying for car repairs. It's from the "sheep pens" that God calls us to higher levels of meaning and significance. That's what happened to King David.

God called David to the palace from the pens. It was in David's lonely, thankless, smelly shepherding work that God ignited the future leader's heart. David learned the art of shepherding sheep and then transferred the principles to people. David's heart of integrity that developed when no one was looking became the same heart of integrity that led a nation to greatness. The skill of nurturing, protecting and caring for sheep became the skill of leading a people to worship God. God developed David in the pens.

Maybe you feel like you are living and working in the "sheep pens." It stinks. It's not particularly pleasant. It's not where you want to be or thought you would be. You feel alone and maybe even abandoned. Let me remind you that God is not wasting your time. Today he is preparing you for tomorrow. Remember: He does his best work in the sheep pens.

Father, give us patience in the pens. Help us learn all you need us to learn so we can be the servants you desire us to be. In Jesus' name. Amen.

JULY 1

Psalm 79:1-7

A psalm of Asaph.

O God, the nations have invaded your inheritance;
    they have defiled your holy temple,
    they have reduced Jerusalem to rubble.
They have left the dead bodies of your servants
    as food for the birds of the sky,
    the flesh of your own people for the animals of the wild.
They have poured out blood like water
    all around Jerusalem,
    and there is no one to bury the dead.
We are objects of contempt to our neighbors,
    of scorn and derision to those around us.

How long, Lord? Will you be angry forever?
    How long will your jealousy burn like fire?
Pour out your wrath on the nations
    that do not acknowledge you,
on the kingdoms
    that do not call on your name;
for they have devoured Jacob
    and devastated his homeland.

Restorer

Today's psalm is a plea for mercy. Jerusalem had been devastated, the temple defiled. Many people of the city had been killed. The surrounding nations now looked at Jerusalem with scorn. In fact, Asaph says, "We are objects of contempt to our neighbors."

The consequences of sin are hard. No one is impressed by the results when we leave God and go our own direction. The price is heavy. Israel was fond of serving Baal and his female counterpart, Asherah. They rejected God despite his warnings. Does God forgive? Yes! Are there still consequences of forgiven sin? Yes!

Maybe the walls of your life have been broken down. Maybe the devastation is self-inflicted. You are experiencing the consequences. It's time to plead for God's mercy. It's time to confess your sins before him. It's time to let him restore and rebuild. Don't give up on God. He has not given up on you.

Father, please hear my prayer. I know my sin and I take full responsibility. You are right in every painful consequence. I now ask for your complete forgiveness. Let me return to the joy I once knew with you. Restore our fellowship and rebuild my life. In Jesus' name. Amen.

JULY 2

Psalm 79:8-13

A psalm of Asaph.

Do not hold against us the sins of past generations;
> may your mercy come quickly to meet us,
> for we are in desperate need.

Help us, God our Savior,
> for the glory of your name;

deliver us and forgive our sins
> for your name's sake.

Why should the nations say,
> "Where is their God?"

Before our eyes, make known among the nations
> that you avenge the outpoured blood of your servants.

May the groans of the prisoners come before you;
> with your strong arm preserve those condemned to die.

Pay back into the laps of our neighbors seven times
> the contempt they have hurled at you, Lord.

Then we your people, the sheep of your pasture,
> will praise you forever;

from generation to generation
> we will proclaim your praise.

Breaking the Cycle

It's called the cycle of sin. A father's absence impacts his son who in turn lives out a pattern of unhealthy relationships. The pain of divorce encourages a daughter to live with her boyfriend to "be sure they can make it together." A child inherits his parents' anemic Christianity and passes it on to his children.

The past impacts the future. Israel knew that well. The sins of their fathers opened the doors for raiding countries to kill and destroy. The sins of the past generation finally opened the door to the Assyrians overthrowing the Northern Kingdom – Israel – and taking them into captivity in 722 BC. The Babylonians did the same with the Southern Kingdom – Judah – in 586 BC.

However, the cycle of sin does not have to continue. By God's grace and strength it can be broken. Your father may not have been present, but your heavenly Father will never leave you nor forsake you. Follow his lead. Your parents may not have stayed together, but God will give you the strength to do marriage the way he intended it. A weak spiritual heritage can be turned into one ignited by Jesus Christ. Let God break the cycle of sin in your life.

Father, please don't hold the sins of the past generation against us. We desire to do things your way. Show us your mercy. Extend your grace. Infuse us with your power. Whatever we have received from our past, help us show faithfulness to those who follow. In Jesus' name. Amen.

JULY 3

Psalm 80:1-7

For the director of music.
To the tune of "The Lilies of the Covenant."
Of Asaph. A psalm.

Hear us, Shepherd of Israel,
    you who lead Joseph like a flock.
You who sit enthroned between the cherubim,
    shine forth before Ephraim, Benjamin and Manasseh.
Awaken your might;
    come and save us.

Restore us, O God;
    make your face shine on us,
    that we may be saved.

How long, Lord God Almighty,
    will your anger smolder
    against the prayers of your people?
You have fed them with the bread of tears;
    you have made them drink tears by the bowlful.
You have made us an object of derision to our neighbors,
    and our enemies mock us.

Restore us, God Almighty;
    make your face shine on us,
    that we may be saved.

God's Smile

Israel was in a dire situation. Enemies had invaded the country and left it devastated. Without God's help they were doomed. Maybe you feel the same way today. Make Asaph's prayer your own.

Restore me. Devastating situations, even those of our own making, knock the props from under our lives. Circumstances set us back in our journeys. Things we built are destroyed. Progress we made is lost. We need restoration.

> *Father, I feel that my life looks like the nation of Israel after the enemies invaded. My home is in disrepair. Relationships have been damaged. My walk with you has been interrupted. I confess my sins before you. Please forgive me. I bring to you the rubble of my life. I ask that you rebuild it. I ask that you restore the joy that I once had living in harmony with you.*

Make your face shine on me. Tough times can make us feel like we are living outside of God's sight. This prayer asks that God show his favor to us and shine on us with his approval.

> *Father, where I am and what I have done has not been in line with your will or instruction. I am sorry. Forgive me. Let me experience your grace. Remind me again that I am your child. Let me feel your favor. Shine your approval on me, not because of who I am, but because of whose I am in Christ. I long to feel your smile on my life again.*
> *In Jesus' name. Amen.*

JULY 4

Psalm 80:8-14a

For the director of music.
To the tune of "The Lilies of the Covenant."
Of Asaph. A psalm.

You transplanted a vine from Egypt;
>*you drove out the nations and planted it.*

You cleared the ground for it,
>*and it took root and filled the land.*

The mountains were covered with its shade,
>*the mighty cedars with its branches.*

Its branches reached as far as the Sea,
>*its shoots as far as the River.*

Why have you broken down its walls
>*so that all who pass by pick its grapes?*

Boars from the forest ravage it,
>*and insects from the fields feed on it.*

Return to us, God Almighty!
>*Look down from heaven and see!*

God Almighty!

The psalmist pictured Israel as a vine that God delivered from Egypt. God cleared the ground and planted them in a new land. The vine took root and spread. There had been a time when Israel flourished and prospered, but then the walls surrounding the vineyard were broken down and others were enjoying its grapes.

There are times in our lives when we think we have everything under control. Like a healthy vine we are flourishing and prospering, but then something hits – illness, breakup, loss, a devastating sin. Those are the times when our cries to God are desperate. Like the psalmist, we pray, "Return to us, God Almighty!" We pray with exclamation marks.

We have One who hears and sympathizes. Jesus understands . . . the weight of temptation, the sting of betrayal, aloneness as he hung on the cross. He is our Mediator who delivers our prayers of exclamation to the Father. Don't give up! Help is on the way.

God Almighty, I need you! The walls of my life are broken down. I am vulnerable to the enemy's attacks. I feel like you have left me. I feel like you have turned your face from me. I feel like I am on my own. I am sinking beneath the weight of life's challenges. Return to me, Lord Almighty! Look down from heaven and see! In Jesus' name. Amen.

JULY 5

Psalm 80:14b-19

For the director of music.
To the tune of "The Lilies of the Covenant."
Of Asaph. A psalm.

Return to us, God Almighty!
    Look down from heaven and see!
Watch over this vine,
    the root your right hand has planted,
    the son you have raised up for yourself.

Your vine is cut down, it is burned with fire;
    at your rebuke your people perish.
Let your hand rest on the man at your right hand,
    the son of man you have raised up for yourself.
Then we will not turn away from you;
    revive us, and we will call on your name.

Restore us, Lord God Almighty;
    make your face shine on us,
    that we may be saved.

Return to Us, God Almighty!

Return to us, God Almighty! Look down from heaven and see! I don't want this marriage to break up. Please work in my spouse's heart. Show me where I need to change.

Return to us, God Almighty! Look down from heaven and see! I am surrounded by people and yet feel so alone. Help me find the perfect peace that results from keeping my focus on you.

Return to us, God Almighty! Look down from heaven and see! Lord, this illness is taking its toll. I am tired and scared. I pray for a good report from the doctor and renewed health.

Return to us, God Almighty! Look down from heaven and see! Father, the job search has been long and fruitless. I am searching and networking and getting very discouraged. Please help me secure the means to support my family.

Return to us, God Almighty! Look down from heaven and see! My child is far from you. I fear for him and the path he is on. I am afraid that he will make some irreversible decisions.

God Almighty, I pray that you will return to your powerful work in my heart. I invite you to take over my life. I want what you have for me. Please look down from heaven, see my desperate state and come to my aid. In Jesus' name. Amen.

JULY 6

Psalm 81:1-10

**For the director of music.
According to gittith. Of Asaph.**

Sing for joy to God our strength;
      shout aloud to the God of Jacob!
Begin the music, strike the timbrel,
      play the melodious harp and lyre.

Sound the ram's horn at the New Moon,
      and when the moon is full, on the day of our festival;
this is a decree for Israel,
      an ordinance of the God of Jacob.
When God went out against Egypt,
      he established it as a statute for Joseph.

I heard an unknown voice say:

"I removed the burden from their shoulders;
      their hands were set free from the basket.
In your distress you called and I rescued you,
      I answered you out of a thundercloud;
      I tested you at the waters of Meribah.
Hear me, my people, and I will warn you –
      if you would only listen to me, Israel!
You shall have no foreign god among you;
      you shall not worship any god other than me.
I am the LORD your God,
      who brought you up out of Egypt.
Open wide your mouth and I will fill it.

Renew Our Passion

Strike up the band! Beat out a rhythm with the percussion. Go crazy on the stringed instruments. Sound the horn! Regardless of how you are feeling it's time to celebrate! Sing from the bottom of your heart and the top of your lungs. Shout loud to the God who is our strength.

Today's focus is not on our problems but on the person of God. He is the one who has delivered us from the slavery of sin. He removed the heavy burden from our shoulders. We called out to him and he rescued us. He is the only God to be honored and worshiped. God will fill our hearts with good things.

Let the party begin. Start the celebration right now, right where you are. Shout out, "God is my strength!" Sing with joy your favorite praise song. Let God know how much you love him by your praise.

Father, help us hold nothing back. Help us get as excited about you as we do our favorite sports team. Help us raise our voices in praise to the God who raised us up from death and gave us eternal life. Renew our passion to praise. In Jesus' name. Amen.

JULY 7

Psalm 81:11-16

For the director of music.
According to gittith. Of Asaph.

But my people would not listen to me;
    Israel would not submit to me.
So I gave them over to their stubborn hearts
    to follow their own devices.

If my people would only listen to me,
    if Israel would only follow my ways,
how quickly I would subdue their enemies
    and turn my hand against their foes!
Those who hate the Lord would cringe before him,
    and their punishment would last forever.
But you would be fed with the finest of wheat;
    with honey from the rock I would satisfy you.

Stubborn Hearts

"If my people would only listen to me . . ." Do you hear God's frustration in this psalm? He wanted to protect Israel and provide for them. He wanted to give them the "finest of wheat" and "honey from the rock." Just as parents want the best for their children, so God desires the best for us – things that bring lasting satisfaction.

Unfortunately, Israel would not listen. They refused to follow God's instruction. They were smarter than him, or so they thought, so he let them follow the dead-end trails of their desires. He let them learn the hard way where their stubborn hearts would lead them.

How about you? You really don't have to learn the hard way. Those lessons are vivid and painful. Sometimes our stubborn sin – even when graciously forgiven – results in irreversible life circumstances. God repeats his plea to us: "If you would only follow my ways I have some great things for you." Jettison the stubborn heart and listen to God.

Father, show us where we are being stubborn and not listening. Soften the hard spots of our hearts. Remind us that your way is always the most satisfying. Thank you for providing and desiring good things for us. In Jesus' name. Amen.

JULY 8

Psalm 82

A psalm of Asaph.

God presides in the great assembly;
> he renders judgment among the "gods":

"How long will you defend the unjust
> and show partiality to the wicked?
Defend the weak and the fatherless;
> uphold the cause of the poor and the oppressed.
Rescue the weak and the needy;
> deliver them from the hand of the wicked.

"The 'gods' know nothing, they understand nothing.
> They walk about in darkness;
> all the foundations of the earth are shaken.

"I said, 'You are "gods";
> you are all sons of the Most High.'
But you will die like mere mortals;
> you will fall like every other ruler."

Rise up, O God, judge the earth,
> for all the nations are your inheritance.

Inaction: Not an Option

When eighteen year olds "age-out" of orphanages in Panama they are left to fend for themselves. Within a year, 70% are in prison, on drugs or involved in prostitution. That's why believers provide help and assistance. We must defend the weak and the fatherless.

The Mathare slum in Nairobi, Kenya is one of the largest in the world. Raw sewage flows in the streets and disease runs rampant through the ten-by-ten shanties crammed side by side. AIDS leaves many children orphaned. Sexual abuse is prevalent. Believers must uphold the cause of the poor and oppressed.

The call to defend the weak and the fatherless, the poor and the oppressed, is a call throughout Scripture. Don't ignore the call. To whom much is given much is expected. Contact your church to find out how you can get involved in rescuing the weak and the needy.

Lord, open our eyes to your instruction and open our hearts to respond. Don't allow inaction to be our response to your call to defend those who can't defend themselves. In Jesus' name. Amen.

JULY 9

Psalm 83:1-8

A song. A psalm of Asaph.

O God, do not remain silent;
    do not turn a deaf ear,
    do not stand aloof, O God.
See how your enemies growl,
    how your foes rear their heads.
With cunning they conspire against your people;
    they plot against those you cherish.
"Come," they say, "let us destroy them as a nation,
    so that Israel's name is remembered no more."

With one mind they plot together;
    they form an alliance against you –
the tents of Edom and the Ishmaelites,
    of Moab and the Hagrites,
Byblos, Ammon and Amalek,
    Philistia, with the people of Tyre.
Even Assyria has joined them
    to reinforce Lot's descendants.

Learning to Pray

I love the honesty that God allows his servants. The Creator who spoke the world into existence desires a personal relationship with us. As part of that intimacy with him he gives us permission to say what's on our hearts.

The psalmist is not disrespectful in his plea. Enemies surround Israel. Like monstrous beasts they "growl" and "rear their heads." They are intent on destruction "so that Israel's name is remembered no more." The psalmist is not questioning God's love. He is simply asking that God get involved in the situation.

We learn to pray in the psalms. Sometimes we praise, sometimes we plead. We share our hearts without pretense. Prayer is not a religious gesture to a deity. It is a heart cry from children to their Father. Prayer is unpretentious communication to the One who loves us so much that he sent his Son to die on our behalf.

Father, I am going to cut the religious jargon. I am going to stop the "thees" and "thous." You are my Father. You bought me from slavery at an unbelievable price – the death of your Son. (Now tell God all that is on your heart.) In Jesus' name. Amen.

JULY 10

Psalm 83:9-18

A song. A psalm of Asaph.

Do to them as you did to Midian,
    as you did to Sisera and Jabin at the river Kishon,
who perished at Endor
    and became like dung on the ground.
Make their nobles like Oreb and Zeeb,
    all their princes like Zebah and Zalmunna,
who said, "Let us take possession
    of the pasturelands of God."

Make them like tumbleweed, my God,
    like chaff before the wind.
As fire consumes the forest
    or a flame sets the mountains ablaze,
so pursue them with your tempest
    and terrify them with your storm.
Cover their faces with shame, Lord,
    so that they will seek your name.

May they ever be ashamed and dismayed;
    may they perish in disgrace.
Let them know that you, whose name is the Lord —
    that you alone are the Most High over all the earth.

The Enemy's Intention

The goal? Comlpete destruction. Time frame? As soon as possible. How? By any and all means of force. The enemies of Israel were on their way. They were coming to wipe the nation off the map; to make the people a chapter in history. They were intent on taking the "pasturelands of God" for their own.

We have an enemy with the same intentions. Satan's goal is total destruction. There is nothing better for his cause than for others to see a believer in the ditch. His time frame is as soon as possible. He wants us out of the picture. He will use anything and everything to destroy us – sexual sin, a failed marriage, questionable business practices, hypocrisy, pretense and our personal sin weaknesses.

Our prayer must be as desperate as the psalmist's. We are no match for Satan on our own. We can resist him only through the power of God. Let's make the psalmist's prayer our own.

Father, the enemy is hot on my trail. Please cover his face with shame so that I can continue to seek your name. May Satan be disgraced. Let him know that you – whose name is the Lord – that you alone are the Most High over all the earth. In Jesus' name. Amen.

JULY 11

Psalm 84:1-7

**For the director of music. According to gittith.
Of the Sons of Korah. A psalm.**

How lovely is your dwelling place,
>   Lord Almighty!
My soul yearns, even faints,
>   for the courts of the Lord;
my heart and my flesh cry out
>   for the living God.
Even the sparrow has found a home,
>   and the swallow a nest for herself,
>   where she may have her young –
a place near your altar,
>   Lord Almighty, my King and my God.
Blessed are those who dwell in your house;
>   they are ever praising you.

Blessed are those whose strength is in you,
>   whose hearts are set on pilgrimage.
As they pass through the Valley of Baka,
>   they make it a place of springs;
>   the autumn rains also cover it with pools.
They go from strength to strength,
>   till each appears before God in Zion.

Power of Community

The psalmist had experienced the power of community. That's why he had a deep desire to go to the temple and meet with God. His whole person cried out "for the living God." God has never been quarantined to one place. He is always available and there is something special about coming together with other believers purposed to praise God.

Certainly the church is not a perfect place. It is full of imperfect people. However, it is God's provision for believers to come together and worship him.

Experiencing the power of community in worship is just as important today as it was for the psalmist. Those who treat going to church lightly treat Jesus lightly. We have to ask and answer the question: Does my soul yearn to worship God in the community of other believers?

Father, never let us take the "Body of Christ," the church, lightly. Help us engage in a community of believers in order to praise you with one heart and one voice. Help us experience the power of community. In Jesus' name. Amen.

JULY 12

Psalm 84:8-12

For the director of music. According to gittith.
Of the Sons of Korah. A psalm.

Hear my prayer, Lord God Almighty;
    listen to me, God of Jacob.
Look on our shield, O God;
    look with favor on your anointed one.

Better is one day in your courts
    than a thousand elsewhere;
I would rather be a doorkeeper in the house of my God
    than dwell in the tents of the wicked.
For the Lord God is a sun and shield;
    the Lord bestows favor and honor;
no good thing does he withhold
    from those whose walk is blameless.

Lord Almighty,
    blessed is the one who trusts in you.

Sun and Shield

The Lord God is a sun. The sun is a revealer. It extinguishes the darkness and allows us to see the world around us. Even when it's overcast, the sun still provides light through the clouds. In the same way, God, the true Light, reveals the path we should take. When our lives are clouded with confusion, pain or grief, his light still shines through.

The Lord God is a shield. We do many things to protect ourselves – insurance, retirement funds, a healthy diet, exercise. All these things are good. However, at end of the day God is the only true source of protection.

No good thing does he withhold . . . A "blameless" walk does not mean perfection. It describes a person whose journey is on God's revealed path. Those who walk close to God experience his constant presence and great blessings. He never holds out on what is best for us.

Father, thank you for your light that shows me where to go, your shield that protects me every moment, your presence on the journey, and the great blessings that you provide all along the way. In Jesus' name. Amen.

JULY 13

Psalm 85:1-7

For the director of music.
Of the Sons of Korah. A psalm.

You, Lord, showed favor to your land;
    you restored the fortunes of Jacob.
You forgave the iniquity of your people
    and covered all their sins.
You set aside all your wrath
    and turned from your fierce anger.

Restore us again, God our Savior,
    and put away your displeasure toward us.
Will you be angry with us forever?
    Will you prolong your anger through all generations?
Will you not revive us again,
    that your people may rejoice in you?
Show us your unfailing love, Lord,
    and grant us your salvation.

The Covering

Forgiveness. What a powerful word! It erases our past from the shame of sin. It releases us to a future of serving God with our whole being. God is a God who forgives. *He covers all my sin.*

Forgiveness. What a beautiful word! God throws our sin into the depths of the sea. He hides it behind his back. He treads it under his foot. He remembers our sin no more. God is a God who forgives. *He covers all my sin.*

Forgiveness. What a cleansing word! I never have to conceal my sin. God sees it all. I can bring my sin to God no matter how fresh, ugly and repulsive it is. God is a God who forgives. *He covers all my sin.*

Forgiveness. What a costly word! Pardon has been made possible through Jesus. He bore my sin in his body on the cross. His agony provided my forgiveness. He died so that I could live. God is a God who forgives. *He covers all my sin.*

Heavenly Father, thank you for being a God who forgives. Thank you for covering all my sin. Thank you for the great forgiveness provided by the work of Jesus. In his name I pray. Amen.

JULY 14

Psalm 85:8-13

For the director of music.
Of the Sons of Korah. A psalm.

I will listen to what God the Lord says;
    he promises peace to his people, his faithful servants –
    but let them not turn to folly.
Surely his salvation is near those who fear him,
    that his glory may dwell in our land.

Love and faithfulness meet together;
    righteousness and peace kiss each other.
Faithfulness springs forth from the earth,
    and righteousness looks down from heaven.
The Lord will indeed give what is good,
    and our land will yield its harvest.
Righteousness goes before him
    and prepares the way for his steps.

Soul Calm

God promises peace to his people. A calm that settles our souls. An anchoring stillness that keeps us steady. An inner balance that keeps us on our feet.

God promises peace to his people. It settles in during sleepless nights. It swoops down during frantic days. It moves our minds from anxiety to the Source of peace.

God promises peace to his people. It comes at the bedside of a sick child. It fills the room of a dying saint. It beats to the rhythm of a monitor in the ICU.

God promises peace to his people. It will not let our minds run wild. It will not leave our hands frozen. It will not leave our hearts beating with fear.

God promises peace to his people. He delivers on all of his promises.

Lord God, you are the author, distributor and sustainer of peace. Thank you for the promise of peace and your provision of it. In Jesus' name. Amen.

JULY 15

Psalm 86:1-7

A prayer of David.

Hear me, Lord, and answer me,
> for I am poor and needy.
Guard my life, for I am faithful to you;
> save your servant who trusts in you.
You are my God; have mercy on me, Lord,
> for I call to you all day long.
Bring joy to your servant, Lord,
> for I put my trust in you.

You, Lord, are forgiving and good,
> abounding in love to all who call to you.
Hear my prayer, Lord;
> listen to my cry for mercy.
When I am in distress, I call to you,
> because you answer me.

Distress Call

David was in a tough situation. He described himself as being "poor and needy." He was in "distress." He cried out for help "all day long." Maybe that's exactly where you are today.

David's requests were many and so were his statements of confidence. He asked God to guard his life, show him mercy and bring him joy. He prayed that God would listen, hear and answer his requests. These requests are shared with his personal God who is "good, abounding in love to all who call" to him. David was confident that his prayer would not go unanswered.

We can have that same confidence. Whatever your situation, God hears your prayer. He is good and abounding in love. He is a God who listens to your cries and has something to give. I don't know how or when God will respond, but I know the answer will be in his perfect time according to his perfect will. That's confidence!

Father, like David, I cry out to you in my distress. Please save your servant who trusts in you. You are forgiving. You are good. You abound in love. I put my trust in you. Thank you for always listening, always hearing and always answering. In Jesus' name. Amen.

JULY 16

Psalm 86:8-13

A prayer of David.

Among the gods there is none like you, Lord;
      no deeds can compare with yours.
All the nations you have made
      will come and worship before you, Lord;
      they will bring glory to your name.
For you are great and do marvelous deeds;
      you alone are God.

Teach me your way, Lord,
      that I may rely on your faithfulness;
give me an undivided heart,
      that I may fear your name.
I will praise you, Lord my God, with all my heart;
      I will glorify your name forever.
For great is your love toward me;
      you have delivered me from the depths,
      from the realm of the dead.

Undivided

Someone has said, "If you are living you are learning." Certainly that is true of those who follow Jesus. Growing believers are always in the process of learning. A growing believer never says, "I know that stuff already."

David was not a spiritual novice when he prayed, "Teach me your way, Lord . . ." His purpose in learning more about God was twofold. First, he wanted his trust in God to expand. He wanted to continually grow in his reliance and dependence on God. Second, he wanted a focused, "undivided" heart so that he could honor God more effectively.

A new day is a new opportunity to learn from God, the perfect Teacher. Let's pray that prayer every morning. Let's ask God to instruct us from his Word and the world around us. Let's ask God every day to expand our dependence and define our focus.

Father, please be my primary teacher today. Instruct me as I take the time to read your Word. Open my eyes to see how you are working in my world and the world at large. Help me grow in my dependence on you. Give me an undivided heart. Help me to honor your name in everything I do. In Jesus' name I pray. Amen.

JULY 17

Psalm 86:14-17

A prayer of David.

Arrogant foes are attacking me, O God;
 ruthless people are trying to kill me –
 they have no regard for you.
But you, Lord, are a compassionate and gracious God,
 slow to anger, abounding in love and faithfulness.
Turn to me and have mercy on me;
 show your strength in behalf of your servant;
save me, because I serve you
 just as my mother did.
Give me a sign of your goodness,
 that my enemies may see it and be put to shame,
 for you, Lord, have helped me and comforted me.

Faithful!

Lord, you are compassionate. Compassion is a deep feeling of sympathy with the desire and ability to do something about it. God's compassion for us sent Jesus to the cross to bear our sins.

Lord, you are gracious. Grace is a free gift with no strings attached. We can't earn it and we don't deserve it.

Lord, you are slow to anger. God knows exactly what we are made of. That is why he is patient with us.

Lord, you are abounding in love. God demonstrated his abounding love in this – while our backs were turned on him he sent his Son to die for us.

Lord, you are faithful. God's promises are true and certain. He will never go back on his word.

Lord, you are merciful. In God's grace he gives us what we don't deserve. In God's mercy he doesn't give us what we do deserve.

Father, thank you for your compassion and grace. Thank you for your patience, love and faithfulness. Thank you for your great mercy – not giving me what my sins deserve. In Jesus' name. Amen.

JULY 18

Psalm 87

Of the Sons of Korah. A psalm. A song.

He has founded his city on the holy mountain.
The Lord loves the gates of Zion
>more than all the other dwellings of Jacob.

Glorious things are said of you,
>city of God:

"I will record Rahab and Babylon
>among those who acknowledge me –

Philistia too, and Tyre, along with Cush –
>and will say, 'This one was born in Zion.'"

Indeed, of Zion it will be said,
>"This one and that one were born in her,
>and the Most High himself will establish her."

The Lord will write in the register of the peoples:
>"This one was born in Zion."

As they make music they will sing,
>"All my fountains are in you."

Chosen

God chose Israel to represent him on earth. Through the nation he showed who he was and how he interacts with those he loves; and through the nation God sent his Son. However, this choosing was not due to Israel's land size or population. God's choosing is always based on his unconditional love (Deuteronomy 7:7-9).

It is still this way with us today. God did not choose you to be his son or daughter because of anything you did or would do. He did not look down through the tunnel of time to evaluate your future performance. We belong to God based solely on his unconditional love.

Think about that amazing fact. In a world of performance, God says, "Grace!" In a world of rewards, God says, "Mercy!" In a world of quotas, God says, "Unconditional." In our temporary existence, God says, "Forever!" In a world that gives only what is earned, God says, "Free!"

Father, thank you for choosing me to be your child. I am sinful, but you forgive me. I am broken, but you heal me. I am lost, but you have found me. I am unworthy, but you have made me worthy through Jesus. In his name I pray. Amen.

JULY 19

Psalm 88:1-9a

A song. A psalm of the Sons of Korah.
For the director of music.
According to mahalath leannoth.
A maskil of Heman the Ezrahite.

L<small>ORD</small>, *you are the God who saves me;*
    day and night I cry out to you.
May my prayer come before you;
    turn your ear to my cry.

I am overwhelmed with troubles
    and my life draws near to death.
I am counted among those who go down to the pit;
    I am like one without strength.
I am set apart with the dead,
    like the slain who lie in the grave,
whom you remember no more,
    who are cut off from your care.

You have put me in the lowest pit,
    in the darkest depths.
Your wrath lies heavily on me;
    you have overwhelmed me with all your waves.
You have taken from me my closest friends
    and have made me repulsive to them.
I am confined and cannot escape;
    my eyes are dim with grief.

Cries in the Night

I wish life was one big party. One whopping celebration. Rich fellowship. Continuous laughter. Good health. Long life. Conflict-free. Prosperity. Days filled with wave after wave of blessing. However . . . the reality is . . . sometimes there are cries in the night.

Twice in today's passage the psalmist says that he is overwhelmed. He is buckling under the weight of his troubles. His strength is gone. He is in the "lowest pit," the "darkest depths." He feels "confined and cannot escape." His eyes are swollen from the tears. Been there?

Challenges are unavoidable as we make our way through this life. Some are as annoying as a dead battery in your car. Some are as awful as an illness stripping the strength from your body. Some leave us overwhelmed, crying out in the night. When we cry out though, God is there. He listens. He hears. He acts. Sometimes he takes away the challenges. Sometimes he works on our overwhelmed souls and replaces the storm with his peace.

Thank you, Father, for hearing my cries in the night. Thank you for reaching down and calming my overwhelmed heart. In Jesus' name. Amen.

JULY 20

Psalm 88:9b-12

A song. A psalm of the Sons of Korah.
For the director of music.
According to mahalath leannoth.
A maskil of Heman the Ezrahite.

I call to you, Lord, every day;
    I spread out my hands to you.
Do you show your wonders to the dead?
    Do their spirits rise up and praise you?
Is your love declared in the grave,
    your faithfulness in Destruction?
Are your wonders known in the place of darkness,
    or your righteous deeds in the land of oblivion?

Trusting With My Questions

For too long we have approached prayer with pretense. We use formulas to make sure we get in "Adoration" before we move to "Confession," "Thanksgiving" and "Supplication." I have used and taught this ACTS method many times, but God is not listening with a checklist making sure we confess before we cry out.

Throughout the psalms, prayers are from the gut, choked out between sobs and cries in the night. Today's prayer begins with a constant call and asks God four rapid-fire questions that can be summed up, "God, how can I praise you if I am dead?!"

I know we like things wrapped up in a nice theological package. We like "five steps" and "six how-to's." That's just not how life works. The answers are not always found in the last verse. Often the psalmist is still feeling the same pain at the end of his prayer as he felt at the beginning. We will see tomorrow that this psalm, like many, ends with more questions than answers. The issue is not getting all of our questions answered. Many times the real issue is trusting God with our questions.

Father, in this life I will not get all my "why's" answered, so please help me to trust you with my questions. In Jesus' name. Amen.

JULY 21

Psalm 88:13-18

A song. A psalm of the Sons of Korah.
For the director of music.
According to mahalath leannoth.
A maskil of Heman the Ezrahite.

But I cry to you for help, Lord;
    in the morning my prayer comes before you.
Why, Lord, do you reject me
    and hide your face from me?

From my youth I have suffered and been close to death;
    I have borne your terrors and am in despair.
Your wrath has swept over me;
    your terrors have destroyed me.
All day long they surround me like a flood;
    they have completely engulfed me.
You have taken from me friend and neighbor –
    darkness is my closest friend.

Heavy in the Morning

You know your heart is heavy when it's heavy in the morning; when the great challenge in your life settles in during your first conscious thoughts; when the dread of another day splashes over your mind before you can splash water on your face.

You know your heart is heavy when it's heavy in the morning; when the cries of the night become the cries of the morning; when the night brought no resolve . . . and no peace.

You know your heart is heavy when it's heavy in the morning; when getting out of bed is labor; when you get dressed unconsciously; when your mind is so filled with that great challenge that nothing else is important.

You know your heart is heavy when it's heavy in the morning; when it feels like God is hiding his face; when the darkness of night is your companion during the day.

You know your heart is heavy when it's heavy in the morning; God knows it too. Your great challenge may still be with you at the end of the day, but God is there too. He desires to carry your heavy load. Hand it over and sleep well.

Father, my heart is heavy. I feel like I have to carry the burden alone. Words like "overwhelmed," "distraught," "exhausted" seem to describe where I am. I am not sure how to let you carry my heavy load, so please show me. Take it from me. Let me rest and be refreshed so that my heart won't be so heavy in the morning. In Jesus' name. Amen.

JULY 22

Psalm 89:1-4

A maskil of Ethan the Ezrahite.

I will sing of the Lord's great love forever;
> with my mouth I will make your faithfulness known
> through all generations.

I will declare that your love stands firm forever,
> that you have established your faithfulness in heaven itself.

You said, "I have made a covenant with my chosen one,
> I have sworn to David my servant,

'I will establish your line forever
> and make your throne firm through all generations.'"

Eternal Echoes

Ethan, the writer of today's psalm, was a Levite (1 Chronicles 15:17-18) and a wise person (1 Kings 4:31). He committed to never stop singing of God's great love and to proclaim God's faithfulness "through all generations." "I will declare," Ethan said, "that your love stands firm forever."

Realizing the brevity of life, how does a person vow to proclaim God's faithfulness "through all generations"? The answer is easy; the application is hard. We must live our lives before our children and grandchildren in such a way that they see the true difference Jesus makes and desire to live godly lives before their children and grandchildren as well.

How you live is what you leave. The impact of one life makes a difference for generations. What we do today echoes into the future. The next generation will stand on our spiritual shoulders . . . or not. The question is this: When you pass away, what will you pass on?

Father, remind us often that our actions impact the future. Remind us that our singular lives are lived in the plural. Guard our thoughts, words, desires and actions. Help us to live today for future impact. In Jesus' name. Amen.

JULY 23

Psalm 89:5-18

A maskil of Ethan the Ezrahite.

The heavens praise your wonders, L<small>ORD</small>,
    your faithfulness too, in the assembly of the holy ones.
For who in the skies above can compare with the L<small>ORD</small>?
    Who is like the L<small>ORD</small> among the heavenly beings?
In the council of the holy ones God is greatly feared;
    he is more awesome than all who surround him.
Who is like you, L<small>ORD</small> God Almighty?
    You, L<small>ORD</small>, are mighty, and your faithfulness surrounds you.

You rule over the surging sea;
    when its waves mount up, you still them.
You crushed Rahab like one of the slain;
    with your strong arm you scattered your enemies.
The heavens are yours, and yours also the earth;
    you founded the world and all that is in it.
You created the north and the south;
    Tabor and Hermon sing for joy at your name.
Your arm is endowed with power;
    your hand is strong, your right hand exalted.

Righteousness and justice are the foundation of your throne;
    love and faithfulness go before you.
Blessed are those who have learned to acclaim you,
    who walk in the light of your presence, L<small>ORD</small>.
They rejoice in your name all day long;
    they celebrate your righteousness.
For you are their glory and strength,
    and by your favor you exalt our horn.
Indeed, our shield belongs to the L<small>ORD</small>,
    our king to the Holy One of Israel.

The Light of His Presence

Everything God does is right. He is pure in thought, desire and action. God can do no wrong. Everything God does is just. His actions are based on his righteousness. His verdict is always true. There is never a hint of impropriety with God.

Because God is righteous and just we can walk in the light of his presence. When we trust in Jesus as the only way to have a personal relationship with the living God, his Spirit indwells us. The Holy Spirit accompanies us on the journey. We are never alone. He illumines our paths with his presence.

God's righteousness, justice and constant presence give the believer reason to celebrate. God is the One we worship. God is the One who gives us strength. God is our shield of protection. We can rejoice in our personal relationship with the living God from sunup to sundown, and throughout eternity.

Father, help us to walk in the light of your presence. There are times when we are tempted by the darkness. The sights and sounds are alluring. We feel pulled from the path. We need your help to stay on the path that is lighted by your presence. Don't let us drift. In Jesus' name. Amen.

JULY 24

Psalm 89:19-29

A maskil of Ethan the Ezrahite.

Once you spoke in a vision,
 to your faithful people you said:
"I have bestowed strength on a warrior;
 I have raised up a young man from among the people.
I have found David my servant;
 with my sacred oil I have anointed him.
My hand will sustain him;
 surely my arm will strengthen him.
The enemy will not get the better of him;
 the wicked will not oppress him.
I will crush his foes before him
 and strike down his adversaries.
My faithful love will be with him,
 and through my name his horn will be exalted.
I will set his hand over the sea,
 his right hand over the rivers.
He will call out to me, 'You are my Father,
 my God, the Rock my Savior.'
And I will appoint him to be my firstborn,
 the most exalted of the kings of the earth.
I will maintain my love to him forever,
 and my covenant with him will never fail.
I will establish his line forever,
 his throne as long as the heavens endure.

An Eternal Throne

King Saul was Israel's first king, followed by King David. While David was far from perfect, he had a tender heart for God. He became the standard for all the kings after him. The kingdom was divided by civil war following David's son, Solomon. However, even with the chaos of the split, God promised that one day the King of Kings would come through David's line.

Matthew started his Gospel with a "record of the genealogy of Jesus Christ the son of David . . . " Both Matthew and Luke show how Jesus came through the house and lineage of David; so the psalmist can say that David's throne will never fail, his line will be forever, and his throne will last "as long as the heavens endure." Jesus will always reign as king.

A study of the Old Testament kings shows a mixed bag of men who were on and off in their commitment to God. Success, and the power that comes with it, brought many a good king, and his kingdom, down, but Jesus changed all of that. He is the true Servant-Leader who humbled himself to death, even death on the cross. Our confidence is this: King Jesus will always be on the throne and reign with righteousness and justice.

Lord Jesus, thank you for being a king who humbled himself. Thank you for taking my sins in your body on the cross. You are the King of Kings and Lord of Lords. Thank you for your work and your reign on my behalf. In your name. Amen.

JULY 25

Psalm 89:30-37

A maskil of Ethan the Ezrahite.

"If his sons forsake my law
    and do not follow my statutes,
if they violate my decrees
    and fail to keep my commands,
I will punish their sin with the rod,
    their iniquity with flogging;
but I will not take my love from him,
    nor will I ever betray my faithfulness.
I will not violate my covenant
    or alter what my lips have uttered.
Once for all, I have sworn by my holiness –
    and I will not lie to David –
that his line will continue forever
    and his throne endure before me like the sun;
it will be established forever like the moon,
    the faithful witness in the sky."

Promised

God promised to preserve the ancestry of David and one day send his Son through that royal line. However many kings who came after David challenged God's great grace and promise.

Solomon's divided heart led to a divided kingdom. After David's son, the nation split in two – Israel in the north and Judah in the south. David's line was preserved through Judah until the birth of Jesus in a Bethlehem manger. The kingdom of Jesus will never end.

God's preservation of David's line is a tremendous demonstration of his sovereign power and commitment to his Word. God swore by his holiness that David's line would continue forever. He will not and cannot lie. Like the sun's ruling of the day and the moon's presence every night, so God will remain faithful to all he has promised.

Father, thank you for your promises. Thank you for keeping every one of them down to the finest detail. Thank you for your faithfulness. I know that you will keep all of your promises to me. In Jesus' name. Amen.

JULY 26

Psalm 89:38-45

A maskil of Ethan the Ezrahite.

But you have rejected, you have spurned,
  you have been very angry with your anointed one.
You have renounced the covenant with your servant
  and have defiled his crown in the dust.
You have broken through all his walls
  and reduced his strongholds to ruins.
All who pass by have plundered him;
  he has become the scorn of his neighbors.
You have exalted the right hand of his foes;
  you have made all his enemies rejoice.
Indeed, you have turned back the edge of his sword
  and have not supported him in battle.
You have put an end to his splendor
  and cast his throne to the ground.
You have cut short the days of his youth;
  you have covered him with a mantle of shame.

Trusting in the Midst of Our Questions

On one hand we know that God's promises are true. On the other hand we know that our challenges are real. Sometimes it's so hard to see how these two can work together. That's what the psalmist was struggling with in this portion of his writing.

God had promised that King David's line would last as long as the heavens endure. God said, "I will maintain my love to him forever, and my covenant with him will never fail." However, here it seemed that God had "rejected" and "renounced" the promise. Enemies had come and "reduced his strongholds to ruins." How could God's promised faithfulness to his people be possible when it seemed that God had not supported them when they needed him most?

This apparent conflict is something we still struggle with today. When illness strikes, discouragement hits, the unwanted divorce occurs, the job goes away, we have to make a move . . . again, we wonder if God has not supported us in our battles. Let's be honest, some days it may feel like that, but God never leaves us. He is always at work behind the scenes weaving a beautiful masterpiece. Someday it will all make sense. Today we continue to trust in the midst of our questions.

Father, sometimes it does feel that you have left us in the battle. We know that you are with us, but so are our feelings of aloneness. The Enemy seems to be taking ground. Our crying out to you seems to go unanswered. We know you are at work, but help us trust you in the midst of our questions. In Jesus' name. Amen.

JULY 27

Psalm 89:46-52

A maskil of Ethan the Ezrahite.

How long, Lord? Will you hide yourself forever?
> How long will your wrath burn like fire?

Remember how fleeting is my life.
> For what futility you have created all humanity!

Who can live and not see death,
> or who can escape the power of the grave?

Lord, where is your former great love,
> which in your faithfulness you swore to David?

Remember, Lord, how your servant has been mocked,
> how I bear in my heart the taunts of all the nations,

the taunts with which your enemies, Lord, have mocked,
> with which they have mocked every step
>
> of your anointed one.

Praise be to the Lord forever!
Amen and Amen.

Death to Life

On my desk to the left of my computer is a *Time* magazine with the cover story, "How to Die." The story, written by Joe Klein, describes the last days in the lives of his mom and dad. I have no problem with the topic, but I do find it strange that this article is explaining how to die without addressing what happens next. OK, maybe I don't find that strange . . . just sad.

Scripture is clear that everyone is going to die. The writer of Hebrews tells us that it is appointed unto men once to die (Hebrews 9:27). No one has power over the day of his death (Ecclesiastes 8:8). Death is indeed the destiny of every man (Ecclesiastes 7:2). However, Scripture is also clear that death is not final. Following death, judgment comes (Hebrews 9:27); and for the believer the judge is our Savior who paid the penalty of our sin and is there to welcome us home.

If you are walking through the last days with someone you love I encourage you to talk openly and honestly about Jesus. Let them know how much he loves them. Let them know that he died for their sins on the cross. Use the time to explain how they can know him and be sure of what happens when they close their eyes in death. Let's not leave it to *Time* magazine to teach us how to die. God's Word is the only place where we find the promise of eternal life. Here are some passages to read and reflect.

> *Very truly I tell you, whoever hears my word and believes him who sent me has eternal life and will not be judged but has crossed over from death to life.* – John 5:24

> *Very truly I tell you, whoever obeys my word will never see death.* – John 8:51

> *Jesus said to her, "I am the resurrection and the life. The one who believes in me will live, even though they die; and whoever lives by believing in me will never die."*
> – John 11:25-26

Father, even when we walk through the valley of the shadow of death, we don't have to fear. Thank you for being with us and giving us courage and comfort. Thank you for carrying us over the bridge that leads from death to life. Thank you in Jesus' name. Amen.

JULY 28

BOOK IV

Psalm 90:1-6

A prayer of Moses the man of God.

Lord, you have been our dwelling place
> throughout all generations.
Before the mountains were born
> or you brought forth the whole world,
> from everlasting to everlasting you are God.

You turn people back to dust,
> saying, "Return to dust, you mortals."
A thousand years in your sight
> are like a day that has just gone by,
> or like a watch in the night.
Yet you sweep people away in the sleep of death –
> they are like the new grass of the morning:
In the morning it springs up new,
> but by evening it is dry and withered.

Everlasting to Everlasting

God is eternal. There was never a time when he wasn't; there will never be a time when he ceases to exist. He has neither beginning nor end.

God is eternal. There is no succession of moments in his being. God never says, "My goodness, I don't know where April went." He is not on a 24 hour cycle of days, weeks, months and years.

God is eternal. He sees all things equally vividly. We see things one moment at a time, but God sees all things from beginning to end at the same time in living color!

God is eternal. While he sees all things equally vividly, God sees events in time and acts in time. He watches me throughout the day. In fact, he never takes his eyes off me. In every situation of my day, God gives me exactly what I need right when I need it.

God is eternal . . . and he loved me so much that he sent his Son to pay the penalty of my sins so I could call him, "Abba, Father." Amazing!

Eternal Father, I cannot comprehend your eternality, but I can experience your love and care. Thank you. In Jesus' name. Amen.

JULY 29

Psalm 90:7-12

A prayer of Moses the man of God.

We are consumed by your anger
    and terrified by your indignation.
You have set our iniquities before you,
    our secret sins in the light of your presence.
All our days pass away under your wrath;
    we finish our years with a moan.
Our days may come to seventy years,
    or eighty, if our strength endures,
yet the best of them are but trouble and sorrow,
    for they quickly pass, and we fly away.
If only we knew the power of your anger!
    Your wrath is as great as the fear that is your due.
Teach us to number our days,
    that we may gain a heart of wisdom.

We Fly Away!

In today's passage, Moses calls for a time of reflection. Our lives, Moses says, "quickly pass, and we fly away." He calls us to consider the brevity of our time on earth. The brevity of life is humbling. C. H. Spurgeon wrote that as people "look into the grave which is soon to be their bed, their passions cool in the presence of mortality . . . "

This solemn reflection about our days on earth allows us to "gain a heart of wisdom." Foolish living focuses only on today and seeks to satisfy immediate desires with instant pleasures. An understanding that our days are ordained by God with no guarantee of tomorrow leads us to invest in things that have eternal value – things that will outlive us.

Wise living comes from the wise investment of our time, gifts and money. One day we will leave all these things behind, but if we use them wisely our investments will continue to pay off. It's not about leaving an inheritance; it's all about leaving a legacy.

Father, we pray with Moses, please teach us to number our days aright. In Jesus' name. Amen.

JULY 30

Psalm 90:13-17

A prayer of Moses the man of God.

Relent, Lord! How long will it be?
    Have compassion on your servants.
Satisfy us in the morning with your unfailing love,
    that we may sing for joy and be glad all our days.
Make us glad for as many days as you have afflicted us,
    for as many years as we have seen trouble.
May your deeds be shown to your servants,
    your splendor to their children.

May the favor of the Lord our God rest on us;
    establish the work of our hands for us –
    yes, establish the work of our hands.

Watch for God

All of us need renewed confirmation. We long to experience God's work . . . again and again. Once is never enough. God's activity in us and around us produces spiritual focus. It allows us to explain the splendor of God to our children. We need to see God at work today . . . and again tomorrow.

Moses was a man who saw God at work. The burning bush, the plagues, the Red Sea, manna from heaven, the Ten Commandments – Moses saw God up close and personal. However, his experiences also taught him how quickly we forget. As he closed this psalm he asked God to continue to show his deeds. God's work would be a review for some and needed first-time learning for their children.

God is at work all around us. He is at work in the nations around the world and in the lives of the people in our world. We need to slow down and watch for him. When we take the time to see his work, we can point it out to our children. We can help them become people who watch for God. That renewed confirmation allows us to be confident in all we do as we establish the work of our hands.

Father, may your deeds be shown to us. May our children marvel at your splendor. May your favor rest on us. Please establish the work of our hands. In Jesus' name. Amen.

JULY 31

Psalm 91:1-8

Whoever dwells in the shelter of the Most High
  will rest in the shadow of the Almighty.
*I will say of the L*ORD*, "He is my refuge and my fortress,*
  my God, in whom I trust."

Surely he will save you
  from the fowler's snare
  and from the deadly pestilence.
He will cover you with his feathers,
  and under his wings you will find refuge;
  his faithfulness will be your shield and rampart.
You will not fear the terror of night,
  nor the arrow that flies by day,
nor the pestilence that stalks in the darkness,
  nor the plague that destroys at midday.
A thousand may fall at your side,
  ten thousand at your right hand,
  but it will not come near you.
You will only observe with your eyes
  and see the punishment of the wicked.

The Shadow of the Almighty

There is a direct connection between where we live and how we live. The things that occupy our minds and drive our hearts will determine the state of our beings. If our greatest concern is money we will be filled with insecurity. If we live in the land of doubt we will experience continual discouragement. Brokenness may be what God uses to get our attention and introduce us to grace, but living there will produce a spiritual self-pity far from the life of spiritual fulfillment that God desires for his children.

When we live in the shelter that God provides, however, we will know a peace that passes all understanding. Living in the "shelter of the Most High" gives us balance with our money, causes inevitable doubt to drive us to the Father for strength, and moves us from brokenness to wholeness in Christ.

Here's the question: Where are you living? Homes of materialism, doubt, brokenness, sexual pleasure, unfaithfulness, pride and inward focus will all come crashing down around you; but when you move into God's shelter you can "rest in the shadow of the Almighty." What are you waiting for? It's time to come home and find rest.

Father, I pray for the person whose mind – whose life – is saturated with the things that result in emptiness. Give them the strength to come home today and dwell in the shelter of the Most High. In Jesus' name. Amen.

AUGUST 1

Psalm 91:9-16

If you say, "The L<small>ORD</small> is my refuge,"
> *and you make the Most High your dwelling,*
no harm will overtake you,
> *no disaster will come near your tent.*
For he will command his angels concerning you
> *to guard you in all your ways;*
they will lift you up in their hands,
> *so that you will not strike your foot against a stone.*
You will tread on the lion and the cobra;
> *you will trample the great lion and the serpent.*

"Because he loves me," says the L<small>ORD</small>, "I will rescue him;
> *I will protect him, for he acknowledges my name.*
He will call on me, and I will answer him;
> *I will be with him in trouble,*
> *I will deliver him and honor him.*
With long life I will satisfy him
> *and show him my salvation."*

Our Refuge and Dwelling

Security. It allows us to live with confidence and peace. We don't know what tomorrow holds, but we know who holds it. Circumstances may churn up our emotions, but the Most High is over all the situations of our lives. God never changes as he works in a world full of constant change. He alone gives us security.

Refuge. Each of us needs to find a place of protection. We are bombarded from all directions. The world attacks from without. The flesh attacks from desires within. At the same time, Satan, a student of our behavior, does his best to hit us between the gaps in our armor – but God is our refuge. He is our place of real protection.

Dwelling. As we journey through the world we need a safe place to stay. We need a place to rest our weary souls. We need encouraging fellowship to build us up. When we make God our dwelling, "no harm will overtake" us. "No disaster will come near" our tents. God will guard us with his angels.

Father, please be my security. I need your confidence and peace. Please be my refuge. I need a place of safety and protection. Please be my dwelling. I need a place to rest on the journey. In Jesus' name. Amen.

AUGUST 2

Psalm 92:1-7

A psalm. A song. For the Sabbath day.

It is good to praise the Lord
       and make music to your name, O Most High,
proclaiming your love in the morning
       and your faithfulness at night,
to the music of the ten-stringed lyre
       and the melody of the harp.

For you make me glad by your deeds, Lord;
       I sing for joy at what your hands have done.
How great are your works, Lord,
       how profound your thoughts!
Senseless people do not know,
       fools do not understand,
that though the wicked spring up like grass
       and all evildoers flourish,
       they will be destroyed forever.

Praising God Together

It is good to come together for worship. Lifting our voices produces both individual and corporate praise. We proclaim the praises of our hearts and honor God with one harmonious voice. Music, always a part of Old Testament worship, is all about proclaiming the love and faithfulness of God.

All true worship is targeted for an audience of One. We are not singing to impress others. Our voices are lifted to the Lord, the Creator God, the Most High. We sing for joy at the great work his hands have done. We confess that his infinite thoughts are beyond our finite understanding.

It's a warning sign when a person says that they have no need to go to church and engage in corporate praise. The Christian life was never meant to be lived solo. We are to come together and sing from the bottoms of our hearts and the tops of our lungs. It is our time to be renewed, refueled, and to praise God with other believers. Praising the Lord and making music to his name inspires us for another week. If you are not engaging in corporate worship you are running low on spiritual fuel.

Father, thank you for the privilege of joining with others to praise you for who you are and what you do. Help us not neglect times of corporate worship. Help us to participate in praise with others. Refuel us in times of worship. In Jesus' name. Amen.

AUGUST 3

Psalm 92:8-15

A psalm. A song. For the Sabbath day.

But you, Lord, are forever exalted.

For surely your enemies, Lord,
> surely your enemies will perish;
> all evildoers will be scattered.

You have exalted my horn like that of a wild ox;
> fine oils have been poured on me.

My eyes have seen the defeat of my adversaries;
> my ears have heard the rout of my wicked foes.

The righteous will flourish like a palm tree,
> they will grow like a cedar of Lebanon;

planted in the house of the Lord,
> they will flourish in the courts of our God.

They will still bear fruit in old age,
> they will stay fresh and green,

proclaiming, "The Lord is upright;
> he is my Rock, and there is no wickedness in him."

The Righteous

The righteous. This is not a description of perfect people or even mostly perfect people. *The righteous* are those who live with a desire and commitment to please God. In the New Testament we have a clearer understanding that our righteousness is made possible by the work of Jesus Christ on the cross.

The righteous, the psalmist says, will be fruitful like a palm tree and strong like a cedar tree. Depending on God for strength, they will flourish. Even old age will not keep them from producing spiritual fruit. They will "stay fresh and green."

The Lord is upright and clothes us with his righteousness. There is no wickedness in his person or his actions. He is unable to do any wrong. He is an unmovable Rock. He is the anchor to which we cling. His righteousness will never be used up or wear out. In Christ we will forever be called *the righteous.*

Father, I stand righteous before you not because of what I have done but because of what you have done for me. Thank you for clothing me with your righteousness now and forever. In Jesus' name. Amen.

AUGUST 4

Psalm 93

The LORD reigns, he is robed in majesty;
    the LORD is robed in majesty and armed with strength;
    indeed, the world is established, firm and secure.
Your throne was established long ago;
    you are from all eternity.

The seas have lifted up, LORD,
    the seas have lifted up their voice;
    the seas have lifted up their pounding waves.
Mightier than the thunder of the great waters,
    mightier than the breakers of the sea –
    the LORD on high is mighty.

Your statutes, LORD, stand firm;
    holiness adorns your house
    for endless days.

Secure on His Throne

The Lord sits securely on his throne. Magnificence envelops him. He is armed with omnipotence.

The Lord sits securely on his throne. He is the ruler over all nations, rulers and people. Under his rule the world is established, firm and secure.

The Lord sits securely on his throne. His reign is not temporary. He does not govern with term limits. His kingship is from eternity past to eternity future.

The Lord sits securely on his throne. The mighty oceans are powerful. Their waves can take down huge ships, crush beachfront property, and flood entire communities. However, God is "mightier than the thunder of the great waters, mightier than the breakers of the sea."

The Lord sits securely on his throne. The grass withers and the flowers fade, but his Word stands firm, set apart "for endless days."

The Lord sits securely on his throne. He is calling the shots. Our King reigns!

Father, thank you for the confidence of knowing that you are now and will forever be on your majestic throne. Thank you that no one or no thing can ever thwart your eternal plan. Thank you for the personal plan that you are working in my life. In Jesus' name. Amen.

AUGUST 5

Psalm 94:1-7

The Lord is a God who avenges.
    O God who avenges, shine forth.
Rise up, Judge of the earth;
    pay back to the proud what they deserve.
How long, Lord, will the wicked,
    how long will the wicked be jubilant?

They pour out arrogant words;
    all the evildoers are full of boasting.
They crush your people, Lord;
    they oppress your inheritance.
They slay the widow and the foreigner;
    they murder the fatherless.
They say, "The Lord does not see;
    the God of Jacob takes no notice."

The Need for Experience

The psalmist would be the first to say that there are times when it seems "The Lord does not see; the God of Jacob takes no notice." The enemy shows up to "crush" God's people, to "oppress" God's inheritance, to "slay the widow", and to "murder the fatherless."

Sometimes it feels like we are alone and on our own. Life hits hard from all sides. We struggle to find our way through the emotional maze. We try to understand how this is going to work out for our good. As we are blasted, the evildoers "are full of boasting."

However, we live life in snapshots, in the pain of the moment – or a string of moments. God sees in video with all the moments weaving perfectly into his master plan. The still shots are painful. One day the divine video will make sense.

Until then, O Lord, we need your help. In the moment it seems like you are absent. We know you are with us, but we have a hard time feeling your presence. Help us today to experience you at work. Move our emotions with the stirring that you are working in our lives. In Jesus' name. Amen.

AUGUST 6

Psalm 94:8-15

Take notice, you senseless ones among the people;
*　　you fools, when will you become wise?*
Does he who fashioned the ear not hear?
*　　Does he who formed the eye not see?*
Does he who disciplines nations not punish?
*　　Does he who teaches mankind lack knowledge?*
The Lord knows all human plans;
*　　he knows that they are futile.*

Blessed is the one you discipline, Lord,
*　　the one you teach from your law;*
you grant them relief from days of trouble,
*　　till a pit is dug for the wicked.*
For the Lord will not reject his people;
*　　he will never forsake his inheritance.*
Judgment will again be founded on righteousness,
*　　and all the upright in heart will follow it.*

Discipline Is Not Rejection

"Blessed is the one you discipline." Doesn't feel like it, does it? But it's true. Discipline is a lifesaver, not only for us but also for those around us.

Discipline will save the life of a child intent on playing by a dangerous street. It is teaching in the most loving form. Discipline demonstrates a love and care that shows we are engaging in our children's lives. Discipline addresses a subject that is harmful in the present and, left unchecked, may be devastating in the future.

Don't mistake discipline for rejection. Rejection ignores the danger. Discipline gets involved. Rejection drives a person away. Discipline draws us near. Rejection ignores. Discipline cares enough to get our attention and provides us safety.

Father, discipline is painful; but thank you for loving us so much that you are willing to work in our lives, get our attention, and bring us back from our dangerous pursuits. Thank you for blessing us with your discipline. In Jesus' name. Amen.

AUGUST 7

Psalm 94:16-23

Who will rise up for me against the wicked?
    Who will take a stand for me against evildoers?
*Unless the L*ORD *had given me help,*
    I would soon have dwelt in the silence of death.
When I said, "My foot is slipping,"
    *your unfailing love, L*ORD*, supported me.*
When anxiety was great within me,
    your consolation brought me joy.

Can a corrupt throne be allied with you –
    a throne that brings on misery by its decrees?
The wicked band together against the righteous
    and condemn the innocent to death.
*But the L*ORD *has become my fortress,*
    and my God the rock in whom I take refuge.
He will repay them for their sins
    and destroy them for their wickedness;
    *the L*ORD *our God will destroy them.*

Waves of Anxiety

Sometimes we can feel it coming on. Like a person who loses his footing on a steep climb, we can feel our emotions slipping. The waves of anxiety build until they crash into our hearts and drench our souls. Here it comes, the fear of uncertainty.

- Your teenager is late coming home on a stormy night.
- Your boss wants to see you first thing in the morning.
- The doctor wants to run some more tests.
- Your mind swirls in the waiting room for news from the surgery.
- The doctor says, "I'm sorry. There is no more we can do."
- The savings are gone.
- Your spouse walks out the door.

Life is filled with things that cause uncertainty. The stuff of life is beyond our control, and it's the lack of control that causes our emotions to implode. What do we do when we are standing in the midst of life and we feel the fear coming on? The psalmist instructs us to turn hard toward God.

It is our loving Father who comes to our aid. As we take on the crashing waves of uncertainty he keeps us standing. When our feet begin to slip, he grabs us and holds on tight. His peace passes human understanding. His comfort brings joy even in the midst of stormy trials. When we know God as our Father, certain help is **always** present with us.

Father, some are reading this with a heart saturated by anxiety. Allow them right now to feel the calming comfort of your Spirit. Give them a certainty of your presence that always comes with a deep peace. Let them know that since you are for us, nothing can stand against us. In Jesus' name. Amen.

AUGUST 8

Psalm 95:1-5

Come, let us sing for joy to the Lord;
   let us shout aloud to the Rock of our salvation.
Let us come before him with thanksgiving
   and extol him with music and song.

For the Lord is the great God,
   the great King above all gods.
In his hand are the depths of the earth,
   and the mountain peaks belong to him.
The sea is his, for he made it,
   and his hands formed the dry land.

Audience of One

Commenting on this psalm, C. H. Spurgeon wrote,

> *Other nations sing unto their gods, let us sing unto Jehovah. We love him, we admire him, we reverence him, let us express our feelings with the choicest sounds, using our noblest faculty for its noblest end. It is well thus to urge others to magnify the Lord, but we must be careful to set a worthy example ourselves, so that we may be able not only to cry "Come," but also to add "let us sing," because we are singing ourselves.*

Worship involves singing to an audience of One. We do not gather to impress others, but to put forth the clarion call of praise. Singing, as Spurgeon said, is the expression of our love, admiration and reverence. Pity the person who has no song to sing to God.

I believe that the most attractive thing an unbeliever can see is a believer truly worshiping the Lord. Put forth the invitation to "Come" and let others see how a person who loves, admires and reveres God expresses their feelings "with the choicest sounds, using our noblest faculty for its noblest end." Don't neglect to sing a song to the audience of One.

Father, thank you for the gift of singing praises to you. May we be those who worship you without worrying about what others think. Help us worship with an audience of One. In Jesus' name. Amen.

AUGUST 9

Psalm 95:6-11

Come, let us bow down in worship,
  let us kneel before the Lord our Maker;
for he is our God
  and we are the people of his pasture,
  the flock under his care.

Today, if only you would hear his voice,
"Do not harden your hearts as you did at Meribah,
  as you did that day at Massah in the wilderness,
where your ancestors tested me;
  they tried me, though they had seen what I did.
For forty years I was angry with that generation;
  I said, 'They are a people whose hearts go astray,
  and they have not known my ways.'
So I declared on oath in my anger,
  'They shall never enter my rest.'"

Slow Down and Bow Down

Busy. That's a word that describes most people I know. Work is packed with meetings, travel and pressure to perform. Families are always on the move to a game, recital or competition. For some families dinnertime is often in the car – fast food in the fast lane.

The psalmist calls for us to slow down. He tells us to bow down and kneel before God. On our knees is not only a posture of reverence; it's a posture of stillness. Driving, walking and running all describe actions of motion, but kneeling shows that I have reached my destination – God's presence.

Slow down and kneel down. Take time for personal worship. Tell God how much you love him. Tell him that this day belongs to him. Tell him that above all else you desire to honor him today in your thoughts, words and actions. It is the critical ingredient in heart preparation. I know that you are busy – too busy not to kneel down and worship.

Father, my calendar is full today. Most of my day I will be running, but right now I kneel and bow before you. I acknowledge you as the Maker of heaven and earth and as my Abba, Father. I desire to live today under your guidance and care. In Jesus' name. Amen.

AUGUST 10

Psalm 96:1-8

Sing to the Lord a new song;
> sing to the Lord, all the earth.

Sing to the Lord, praise his name;
> proclaim his salvation day after day.

Declare his glory among the nations,
> his marvelous deeds among all peoples.

For great is the Lord and most worthy of praise;
> he is to be feared above all gods.

For all the gods of the nations are idols,
> but the Lord made the heavens.

Splendor and majesty are before him;
> strength and glory are in his sanctuary.

Ascribe to the Lord, all you families of nations,
> ascribe to the Lord glory and strength.

Ascribe to the Lord the glory due his name;
> bring an offering and come into his courts.

The Living God

Israel was surrounded by nations that worshiped false gods. Baal, and his female counterpart, Asherah, were prominent among the Canaanites. The Phoenicians worshiped Beel-Zebul and the Moabites worshiped Chemish. The Philistines had Dagon, the Arameans, Hadad, and the Babylonians, Marduk. The Ammonites bowed before Molech who demanded human sacrifices.

These gods, however, were man-made, constructed of wood and stone. Jeremiah likened them to a "scarecrow in a cucumber field." They could not speak and had to be carried because they could not walk. The gods of the nations were powerless, but not the God of Israel.

The Lord is God and he is great. He is most worthy of our praise. He is to be honored, worshiped, and obeyed. He is the Creator God who made the heavens. He is the all-powerful God that created man. He is the living God who works in history. He is the personal God who sent his Son to pay the penalty of our sin so we could have an eternal relationship with him.

Father, you are the living God. We worship you and you alone. Show us if we are worshiping anything besides you. Help us put that god out of our lives. Help us to give you the glory that you deserve. In Jesus' name. Amen.

AUGUST 11

Psalm 96:9-13

Worship the Lord in the splendor of his holiness;
> tremble before him, all the earth.

Say among the nations, "The Lord reigns."
> The world is firmly established, it cannot be moved;
> he will judge the peoples with equity.

Let the heavens rejoice, let the earth be glad;
> let the sea resound, and all that is in it.

Let the fields be jubilant, and everything in them;
> let all the trees of the forest sing for joy.

Let all creation rejoice before the Lord, for he comes,
> he comes to judge the earth.

He will judge the world in righteousness
> and the peoples in his faithfulness.

True Worship

Worship is something I do. It is an active demonstration of my love for God by appropriately responding to his person, work and Word. Worship is responding to the God who loves me so much that he sent his Son to pay the penalty for my sins. Worship is responding in thanksgiving to the work that God does in my life. Worship is responding in obedience to God's Word – his love letter to me.

Worship is both private and public. When we gather and express our love to God with other believers, there is great encouragement in knowing that we are not alone in the Christian life. When I am alone with God there is a special time of sharing my heart – praise, thanksgiving, fears, desires, needs, dreams – with him.

Worship is not confined to our daily devotional time or attendance at a weekend service, however. Worship is the believer's way of life. Showing kindness to a neighbor is just as much worship as singing great songs of praise to God at the top of my lungs. Worship is an active demonstration of my love for God . . . even when no one else is looking.

Father, help us to be true worshipers in every aspect of our lives. In Jesus' name. Amen.

AUGUST 12

Psalm 97:1-7

The Lord reigns, let the earth be glad;
    let the distant shores rejoice.
Clouds and thick darkness surround him;
    righteousness and justice are the
    foundation of his throne.
Fire goes before him
    and consumes his foes on every side.
His lightning lights up the world;
    the earth sees and trembles.
The mountains melt like wax before the Lord,
    before the Lord of all the earth.
The heavens proclaim his righteousness,
    and all peoples see his glory.

All who worship images are put to shame,
    those who boast in idols –
    worship him, all you gods!

Coming Judgment

The Psalms are filled with songs of praise and thanksgiving. These passages lift our spirits and encourage our hearts. The Psalms also contain teaching about God's judgment. Today's passage expresses this solemn truth.

Clouds and thick darkness are pictures of God's awesome judgment. God's reign is based on righteousness (everything he does is right) and justice (everything he does is fair). The fire, the lightning, the trembling, the melting like wax show that he is not one to trifle with. All will see God in all of his glory. Those who worship idols will be put to shame.

Scripture says that it is appointed unto man once to die and after that the judgment (Hebrews 10:27). One day every knee will bow to proclaim that Jesus is Lord (Philippians 2:11). The judgment is coming. The question is: Are you ready? If you would like to be sure, make the following prayer your own.

Lord, I know that I will die one day and then stand before you. I want to stand before you as your son/daughter. Today I trust in Jesus, who paid for my sin on the cross. I trust in Jesus as the One who took my judgment in his body on the cross. I trust in Jesus alone as the only way to have an eternal relationship with you – the One who is righteous and just. In Jesus' name. Amen.

AUGUST 13

Psalm 97:8-12

Zion hears and rejoices
    and the villages of Judah are glad
    because of your judgments, Lord.
For you, Lord, are the Most High over all the earth;
    you are exalted far above all gods.
Let those who love the Lord hate evil,
    for he guards the lives of his faithful ones
    and delivers them from the hand of the wicked.
Light shines on the righteous
    and joy on the upright in heart.
Rejoice in the Lord, you who are righteous,
    and praise his holy name.

Hating the Right Thing

Many times our emotions are riled by things that are not really that important. We get angry when we're stuck in traffic. We get ticked off when our car won't start or our garage door opener quits working. We fume when an automated answering message leads us on a wild goose chase. Think about the last thing that revved up your emotions. Was it worth all that emotion?

Believers are called to pour out their passion against one thing – evil. "Let those who love the Lord hate evil." "Evil" describes the sexual sins that lead to prostitution, sex trafficking and rape. "Evil" describes governments starving their people and rampages of ethnic cleansing. "Evil" describes the persecution and killing of Christians around the world.

But don't stop there. We should also hate and avoid the evil that desires to trap and destroy us. Envy, jealousy, hatred, adultery, addictions, pornography, breaking of vows, lying, stealing, and . . . the list goes on. We must hate the evil in our own lives as much as we hate the evil we see in the world.

Father, shine your light on our passions. Show us if our emotions are spent on the right things. Help us recognize evil in our own lives. Help us to hate it. Help us to uproot it. Help us walk in the light of the right path and experience your joy all along the way. In Jesus' name. Amen.

AUGUST 14

Psalm 98:1-3

Sing to the LORD a new song,
for he has done marvelous things;
his right hand and his holy arm
have worked salvation for him.
The LORD has made his salvation known
and revealed his righteousness to the nations.
He has remembered his love
and his faithfulness to Israel;
all the ends of the earth have seen
the salvation of our God.

Staying Unstuck

Many years ago we had Sunday evening services at our church where people could stand up and share a short devotion. Every year a man, visiting his family, would attend a service and share from Scripture. The first time I heard him I was impressed. He took an obscure passage of the Old Testament and made it come alive. On the following year's visit, he shared the same passage. The next year . . . same passage. Then the next year . . . same passage. The first year I likened the visitor to a Bible-teaching John Wayne. By year five I saw him as Barney Fife. The guy had only one teaching bullet!

I have seen more than one person get stuck in a spiritual rut. Every time you talk with them God is "teaching them" from the same passage. They praise God for the same things, struggle with the same sin, and ask the same questions. Like the high school athlete still talking about that touchdown run to win the championship 40 years ago, some believers are stuck in time; but look at today's passage. It is time to "sing to the Lord a new song."

God's past faithfulness gives me confidence. God's future promises give me hope. However, it is God's work in my life today that refreshes my relationship with him. Look around you! God is doing marvelous things in your life. He is moving you forward with spiritual victories. He is stretching you with challenging times. He is causing you to depend on him for strength. Today he is forming you into what he needs you to be tomorrow. His mercies are new every morning. It's time to sing a new song!

Father, please don't let us get stuck in a spiritual rut. Refresh us for the journey today, and put a new song in our hearts! In Jesus' name. Amen.

AUGUST 15

Psalm 98:4-9

Shout for joy to the LORD all the earth,
　　burst into jubilant song with music;
make music to the LORD with the harp,
　　with the harp and the sound of singing,
with trumpets and the blast of the ram's horn –
　　shout for joy before the LORD, the King.

Let the sea resound, and everything in it,
　　the world, and all who live in it.
Let the rivers clap their hands,
　　let the mountains sing together for joy;
let them sing before the LORD,
　　for he comes to judge the earth.
He will judge the world in righteousness
　　and the peoples with equity.

Crazy Crowd Praise

My family and I live in Pittsburgh, and when it's kickoff time at Heinz Field the sound is deafening. When the Steelers score a touchdown there is dancing in the aisles. When the Pirates are in the playoffs the PNC crowd is crazy. Most people leave with gravelly voices from yelling at the top of their lungs for three hours. This psalm reminds us that God wants and deserves just as much passion and energy in worship.

C. H. Spurgeon wrote, "Every tongue must applaud, and that with the vigour which joy of heart alone can arouse to action. As men shout when they welcome a king, so must we . . . Beware of singing as if you were half dead or half asleep . . . lift up your voice with strength."

Shout for joy to the Lord! Burst into jubilant song! Sing from the bottom of your heart and the top of your lungs. Don't sing as if you were half dead or half asleep. It's time to make some noise for the Lord, the King.

Father, help me get excited about things that are important to you. Help me praise you passionately with all my heart and with all my being. In Jesus' name. Amen.

AUGUST 16

Psalm 99:1-5

The LORD reigns,
   let the nations tremble;
he sits enthroned between the cherubim,
   let the earth shake.
Great is the LORD in Zion;
   he is exalted over all the nations.
Let them praise your great and awesome name –
   he is holy.

The King is mighty, he loves justice –
   you have established equity;
in Jacob you have done
   what is just and right.
Exalt the LORD our God
   and worship at his footstool;
   he is holy.

He Is Holy

Twice in this passage the psalmist writes that God is holy. God's holiness means that he is completely separated from sin. He is perfect in his person, words and actions. God is alone in his holiness. There is no one like him.

That's why the psalmist exhorts us to praise God's great and awesome name. That's why we are to exalt him and worship him. He reigns over all people and nations. He is powerful and "loves justice." He always does what is just and right. There never has been and never will be a hint of evil in anything he says or does.

Now, for the time being, set aside your requests. Praise God for who he is. Praise him for his great holiness. Praise him for the fact that there is no one like him. "The King is mighty." Praise him for his righteousness and justice. Applaud the great God who loves you so much that he sent Jesus to die on the cross for your sins. Through the work of Jesus the holy God has made us holy (Hebrews 10:10)! Praise the Lord!

Thank you, Father, for your holiness. Thank you for your greatness. I praise you because you are the mighty King. I praise you for your loving justice and equity. I praise your great and awesome name. Thank you that through Jesus I stand holy in your sight. In his name I pray. Amen.

AUGUST 17

Psalm 99:6-9

Moses and Aaron were among his priests,
> Samuel was among those who called on his name;

they called on the Lord
> and he answered them.

He spoke to them from the pillar of cloud;
> they kept his statutes and the decrees he gave them.

Lord our God,
> you answered them;

you were to Israel a forgiving God,
> though you punished their misdeeds.

Exalt the Lord our God
> and worship at his holy mountain,
> for the Lord our God is holy.

Our God Is Holy

In this psalm the writer drives home the point that God is holy. There is no one like him. He is set apart from all others. This truth is expressed in verses three and five, then in the final verse as an exclamation – "for the Lord our God is holy." However, God's holiness – his set apartness – does not mean that he is unreachable.

Moses, Aaron and Samuel were three examples of God's personal relationship with man. These mere men called on the Lord. They spoke to the holy God, and he heard them! God listened to mere men express their hearts and he answered them!

What an amazing truth! We can speak to the holy God as we would speak with a friend. He will never be too busy. He will never be preoccupied. God will always listen when you call on him. He will always answer in his perfect time according to his perfect will. Call on God right now and tell him all that is on your heart.

Father, thank you for listening to my prayer. Here are the things that are on my heart today…

AUGUST 18

Psalm 100

A psalm. For giving grateful praise.

Shout for joy to the Lord, all the earth.
> Worship the Lord with gladness;
> come before him with joyful songs.

Know that the Lord is God.
> It is he who made us, and we are his;
> we are his people, the sheep of his pasture.

Enter his gates with thanksgiving
> and his courts with praise;
> give thanks to him and praise his name.

For the Lord is good and his love endures forever;
> his faithfulness continues through all generations.

Shout for Joy

I confess that my prayers are too often heavy on petition and weak on praise. Today's passage reminds us to enter his presence with thanksgiving and explains why God alone is worthy of our praise. Let's break it down.

> **Shout for joy to the Lord.** Heartfelt thanksgiving involves a gratitude that cannot be held back or held in. We shout for joy when our favorite team scores, so how much more should we loudly express the emotion that comes with experiencing the living God at work in our lives?
>
> **Worship the Lord with gladness.** Worship is not comprised of singing a few songs at a church service. Demonstrating that God is worthy of my adoration is something I must do all day every day.
>
> **Come before him with joyful songs.** My dad used to say that he "couldn't carry a tune in a bucket." I'm in the same boat. However, God is not concerned about the tune of my voice; he's focused on the tune of my heart. God made us to sing joyful songs from the depths of our beings.
>
> **Know that the Lord is God.** We belong to the one and only Maker of heaven and earth, who loves us so much that he sent his Son to die for our sins. Because of Jesus "we are his people!" That truth alone deserves a shout for joy, joyous worship and the singing of some joyful songs!

Father, forgive me for being lite on thanksgiving. I am truly sorry. Beginning today, help me to be a more consistent and emotional giver of thanks. In Christ's name. Amen.

AUGUST 19

Psalm 101

Of David. A psalm.

I will sing of your love and justice;
    to you, Lord, I will sing praise.
I will be careful to lead a blameless life –
    when will you come to me?

I will conduct the affairs of my house
    with a blameless heart.
I will not look with approval
    on anything that is vile.

I hate what faithless people do;
    I will have no part in it.
The perverse of heart shall be far from me;
    I will have nothing to do with what is evil.

Whoever slanders their neighbor in secret,
    I will put to silence;
whoever has haughty eyes and a proud heart,
    I will not tolerate.

My eyes will be on the faithful in the land,
    that they may dwell with me;
the one whose walk is blameless
    will minister to me.

No one who practices deceit
    will dwell in my house;
no one who speaks falsely
    will stand in my presence.

Every morning I will put to silence
    all the wicked in the land;
I will cut off every evildoer
    from the city of the Lord.

Renewing Our Commitments

Sometimes it's time for renewed commitments. These times may follow a bad decision, a time away from God or a feeling of apathy. Sometimes we are stuck in blatant sin like a helpless man trapped in quicksand. Like the prodigal son we come to our senses. It's time to get serious.

In today's psalm, King David made some thoughtful pledges. David was determined to conduct the affairs of his house with a pure heart. He made a covenant with his eyes to turn from anything abhorrent. He hated the God-dishonoring actions of the people around him.

Maybe it's time for you to renew some commitments to God. You have been away too long. You've been hanging out with the wrong people. You have put your stamp of approval on things opposed to God. Today is the day to slow down, hit the pause button and refresh your walk with God.

Father, I have been gone too long. Please forgive me for distancing myself from you and for the sin that distance brings. Hear my renewed commitments and give me the strength to follow through. In Jesus' name. Amen.

AUGUST 20

Psalm 102:1-11

A prayer of an afflicted person who has grown weak and pours out a lament before the Lord.

Hear my prayer, Lord;
  let my cry for help come to you.
Do not hide your face from me
  when I am in distress.
Turn your ear to me;
  when I call, answer me quickly.

For my days vanish like smoke;
  my bones burn like glowing embers.
My heart is blighted and withered like grass;
  I forget to eat my food.
In my distress I groan aloud
  and am reduced to skin and bones.
I am like a desert owl,
  like an owl among the ruins.
I lie awake; I have become
  like a bird alone on a roof.
All day long my enemies taunt me;
  those who rail against me use my name as a curse.
For I eat ashes as my food
  and mingle my drink with tears
because of your great wrath,
  for you have taken me up and thrown me aside.
My days are like the evening shadow;
  I wither away like grass.

A Bird Alone on a Roof

Life delivers striking blows. Staggering shots. Jolts that slam on the brakes and bring us to a screeching halt. Separation. Divorce. A prodigal child. Death. Grief. An illness that takes us down. These things overwhelm our emotions and take over our minds. While the world speeds by, we live in what seems like a state of slow motion.

Today's psalm is the "prayer of an afflicted person who has grown weak and pours out a lament before the Lord." The writer cries out for help. "God, please do not hide your face from me." "Lord, I have to have an answer now!" The burden is so all-consuming that the natural craving for food is forgotten.

Can you relate to the psalmist? Can you relate to the cries, pleading and groans? Do you feel like the psalmist – "a bird alone on a roof"? This is not the end of the psalm. We will continue the prayer tomorrow; but for today, pour out all that is on your heart. Let God know how you feel – scared, exhausted, overwhelmed, alone. Your raw honesty will open your heart to hear his voice. He is there with you and will never leave.

Father, today life feels painful. I cry out to you. Sometimes I don't even know what to say, so I share my raw heart. I long for your intervention and your peace. In Jesus' name. Amen.

AUGUST 21

Psalm 102:12-17

A prayer of an afflicted person who has grown weak and pours out a lament before the Lord.

But you, Lord, sit enthroned forever;
> your renown endures through all generations.

You will arise and have compassion on Zion,
> for it is time to show favor to her;
> the appointed time has come.

For her stones are dear to your servants;
> her very dust moves them to pity.

The nations will fear the name of the Lord,
> all the kings of the earth will revere your glory.

For the Lord will rebuild Zion
> and appear in his glory.

He will respond to the prayer of the destitute;
> he will not despise their plea.

A Bird Alone on a Roof (Continued)

This psalm was written by an afflicted person who had grown weak. This person poured out his heart to the Lord. In the first part of the prayer, this servant was worn down. His personal challenges were crushing. He was wasting away – body and soul. He felt "like a bird alone on a roof."

However, in today's passage he turned his thoughts to the person of God. In contrast to his vulnerability, the Lord sits "enthroned forever." God remains the same throughout all generations. His work in the past proves that he will work in the present. The love he has for his people will never fade or fail.

Do you feel like the psalmist – "a bird alone on a roof"? This passage reminds us to steady our hearts with the person of God. While our world crumbles down around us, he remains "enthroned forever." He endures. He never leaves us alone on a roof.

Father, in the midst of my devastation I turn my focus to you – the One who sits enthroned forever. The One whose reputation and fame withstand time and change. I choose to trust you, not my present circumstance. Hear my prayer and come my aid. I pray in Jesus' name. Amen.

AUGUST 22

Psalm 102:18-28

A prayer of an afflicted person who has grown weak and pours out a lament before the Lord.

Let this be written for a future generation,
> that a people not yet created may praise the Lord:
"The Lord looked down from his sanctuary on high,
> from heaven he viewed the earth,
to hear the groans of the prisoners
> and release those condemned to death."
So the name of the Lord will be declared in Zion
> and his praise in Jerusalem
when the peoples and the kingdoms
> assemble to worship the Lord.

In the course of my life he broke my strength;
> he cut short my days.
So I said:
"Do not take me away, my God, in the midst of my days;
> your years go on through all generations.
In the beginning you laid the foundations of the earth,
> and the heavens are the work of your hands.
They will perish, but you remain;
> they will all wear out like a garment.
Like clothing you will change them
> and they will be discarded.
But you remain the same,
> and your years will never end.
The children of your servants will live in your presence;
> their descendants will be established before you."

A Bird Alone on a Roof (Continued)

This psalm was written by a person going through an extremely challenging time. The beginning of the psalm gives this description: "The prayer of an afflicted person who has grown weak and pours out a lament before the Lord." He felt "like a bird alone on a roof." After pouring out his heart in the first 11 verses, in verses 12-17 the focus is turned to God, who is "enthroned forever." Now the prayer is concluded by zooming in on two attributes of God.

> **God is immutable.** The world, and our world, is in constant change. For us change can range from desired to devastating, but God never changes. As he was in the beginning, so he is today. He remains the same.

> **God is eternal.** There was never a time when God was not. There will never be a time when God is not. We "wear out like a garment," but God's time will never end.

When our world is rocked, God is the solid rock that never moves, changes or goes away. That gives us confidence. Our trust is in the One whose promises are true, whose power is unlimited, and whose love never ends. Hold onto the immutable, eternal God. He will hold onto you forever.

Father, you never change! You are eternal! Help me keep my focus on you and not on the stuff around me. I thank you for the promises that I can cling to today, and I thank you that my children can cling to those same promises. Help me live in a way that encourages future generations to praise you. In Jesus' name. Amen.

AUGUST 23

Psalm 103:1-12

Of David.

Praise the L<small>ORD</small>, my soul;
    all my inmost being, praise his holy name.
Praise the L<small>ORD</small>, my soul,
    and forget not all his benefits –
who forgives all your sins
    and heals all your diseases,
who redeems your life from the pit
    and crowns you with love and compassion,
who satisfies your desires with good things
    so that your youth is renewed like the eagle's.

The L<small>ORD</small> works righteousness
    and justice for all the oppressed.

He made known his ways to Moses,
    his deeds to the people of Israel:
The L<small>ORD</small> is compassionate and gracious,
    slow to anger, abounding in love.
He will not always accuse,
    nor will he harbor his anger forever;
he does not treat us as our sins deserve
    or repay us according to our iniquities.
For as high as the heavens are above the earth,
    so great is his love for those who fear him;
as far as the east is from the west,
    so far has he removed our transgressions from us.

Limitless Love

In Christ we are significant, secure, accepted, forgiven and empowered. God loves us so much that he sent his Son to die for our sins and that love continues to embrace every day of our spiritual journeys. In his book *The Knowledge of the Holy,* A. W. Tozer helps us understand the extent of God's great love.

> ***God's Word assures us that he desires to be our friend.*** Tozer says, "No man with a trace of humility would first think that he is a friend of God; but the idea did not originate with men." God himself said that Abraham was his friend, and he desires the same friendship with us.
>
> ***Love is an emotional identification.*** Tozer writes, "It is a strange and beautiful eccentricity of the free God that He has allowed His heart to be emotionally identified with men. Self-sufficient as He is, He wants our love and will not be satisfied till He gets it. Free as He is, He has let His heart be bound to us forever."
>
> ***Love takes pleasure in its object.*** "The Lord," Tozer says, "takes peculiar pleasure in His saints . . . Christ in His atonement has removed the bar to the divine fellowship. Now in Christ all believing souls are objects of God's delight."

It's hard to imagine such an all-encompassing love. We know our sin and failure, yet God continues to embrace us with his love and forgiveness. How do we respond to such unconditional compassion?

Heavenly Father, thank you for loving me. Thank you for loving me when I am unlovable. Thank you for forgiving my sin and failure. Thank you for a relationship with you through Jesus. Thank you for calling me your friend. In Jesus' name. Amen.

AUGUST 24

Psalm 103:13-18

Of David.

As a father has compassion on his children,
> so the Lord has compassion on those who fear him;

for he knows how we are formed,
> he remembers that we are dust.

The life of mortals is like grass,
> they flourish like a flower of the field;

the wind blows over it and it is gone,
> and its place remembers it no more.

But from everlasting to everlasting
> the Lord's love is with those who fear him,
> and his righteousness with their children's children –

with those who keep his covenant
> and remember to obey his precepts.

Limitless Love (Continued)

In his book *The Knowledge of the Holy,* A. W. Tozer writes, "Love is an essential attribute of God." Tozer explains that all of God's attributes are always at work together. One is never held back in order to emphasize another. Let's think about what that means.

God is eternal, so his love has no beginning or end. There has never been a time when God wasn't, so his love has always existed. There will never be a time when God ceases to exist, so his love will always exist. It is from everlasting to everlasting.

God is infinite, so his love has no limits. God's love is not restricted by capacity. His love has no boundaries or stopping point. There will never be a time when God quits loving us.

God is holy, so his love is pure. On our best day, our love is tainted by our sinfulness. However, God's love and his motives are completely pure. God's love for us is perfect.

I don't know what you are going through today, but I do know this: God loves you! He loves you with an everlasting love. God loves you! He loves you with a limitless love. He will never stop loving you. God loves you! His motivation in loving you is pure. He paid a great price to redeem you from sin's slavery. You are significant. You are secure. You are accepted. You are forgiven. You are empowered. You are a child of the living God all because of his great love.

Father, thank you for your eternal, limitless and pure love. Help me respond with a life of thanksgiving and honor demonstrated by obedience in all the areas of my life. In Jesus' name. Amen.

AUGUST 25

Psalm 103:19-22

Of David.

*The L*ORD *has established his throne in heaven,*
    and his kingdom rules over all.

*Praise the L*ORD*, you his angels,*
    you mighty ones who do his bidding,
    who obey his word.
*Praise the L*ORD*, all his heavenly hosts,*
    you his servants who do his will.
*Praise the L*ORD*, all his works*
    everywhere in his dominion.

*Praise the L*ORD*, my soul.*

Responding to Limitless Love

I was reflecting on my prayer life recently and concluded that I have been doing more whining than praying. I was focused on letting God know that he was slow in delivering my wants and that he was holding back on my desires. My conversation was one way and consisted of statements in the form of questions like, "God, what are you doing?" I have been talking at God instead of with him.

This psalm gave me needed pause and perspective. In the first eighteen verses David declares the limitless love of the eternal God who takes our sin and separates it as far as the east is from the west. This God is the very One whose "kingdom rules over all." Make no mistake, he is God and he is in charge. How am I to respond to such a loving and great God? Quit whining and start praising!

David concludes this psalm by declaring that all the angels, all creation and all God's servants should praise the Lord. He closes this psalm in the same way he started it. David exhorts himself ("my soul") to live a life of praise. As children of God, we must exhort ourselves to do the same.

Father, thank you for allowing me to pour my heart out to you – my wants and desires. But don't let me turn my conversation with you into a time of whining. Help me to praise you for who you are and how you are at work in my life. In Jesus' name. Amen.

AUGUST 26

Psalm 104:1-9

Praise the Lord, my soul.

Lord my God, you are very great;
> you are clothed with splendor and majesty.

The Lord wraps himself in light as with a garment;
> he stretches out the heavens like a tent
> and lays the beams of his upper chambers
> on their waters.

He makes the clouds his chariot
> and rides on the wings of the wind.

He makes winds his messengers,
> flames of fire his servants.

He set the earth on its foundations;
> it can never be moved.

You covered it with the watery depths as with a garment;
> the waters stood above the mountains.

But at your rebuke the waters fled,
> at the sound of your thunder they took to flight;

they flowed over the mountains,
> they went down into the valleys,
> to the place you assigned for them.

You set a boundary they cannot cross;
> never again will they cover the earth.

The Person of God

Perhaps the writer of today's psalm felt the danger of self-focus. Maybe he realized the need to get beyond himself and turn his attention to God. Whatever his circumstances he pushed himself to praise. Like a coach yelling encouragement from the sidelines, he encouraged himself (his soul) to "praise the Lord."

Praising the Lord is not something we conjure up. Notice that the psalmist bases his worship on the person of God. He reminds himself that God is great and majestic. He is the One who "set the earth on its foundations." The psalmist prodded himself to praise by reminding himself of God's person and work.

It is easy to become self-focused. Life hits hard from every direction. Sometimes we withdraw into ourselves to provide needed protection. We put up an emotional shield to defend against painful arrows. The stuff of life often leads us to a place of self-centeredness. This is not unnatural. However, when we stay there too long . . . that's when it gets dangerous. Today it's time for self-exhortation: Praise the Lord, my soul!

Father, coach us by your Spirit to praise you. Help us turn from a self-focus to a life of praise. As we read your Word remind us of who you are and how you work in our lives. Help us to be people of praise. In Jesus' name. Amen.

AUGUST 27

Psalm 104:10-18

He makes springs pour water into the ravines;
> it flows between the mountains.

They give water to all the beasts of the field;
> the wild donkeys quench their thirst.

The birds of the sky nest by the waters;
> they sing among the branches.

He waters the mountains from his upper chambers;
> the land is satisfied by the fruit of his work.

He makes grass grow for the cattle,
> and plants for people to cultivate –
> bringing forth food from the earth:

wine that gladdens human hearts,
> oil to make their faces shine,
> and bread that sustains their hearts.

The trees of the Lord are well watered,
> the cedars of Lebanon that he planted.

There the birds make their nests;
> the stork has its home in the junipers.

The high mountains belong to the wild goats;
> the crags are a refuge for the hyrax.

Note to Self: Praise God Today!

This psalm begins with the self-exhortation: "Praise the Lord, my soul." It is a note to self – get your focus off you and on God! If you are searching for praiseworthy things, this portion of the psalm takes you back to the basics.

Water. This colorless, transparent, odorless, tasteless liquid is the basis of the fluids in living organisms. Water is essential. Assuming that you are in fairly good shape, you could live only four to six days without this essential compound made up of two atoms of hydrogen and one atom of oxygen. This liquid, that many of us take for granted, comes from the hand of the gracious God.

If you are having trouble praising God, start with water. Thank God that he sees fit to provide you with all the water you need. Thank him for the rain, springs and rivers. Thank him that the "land is satisfied by the fruit of his work." He loves us so much that he takes care of the essentials. And . . . he can take care of everything else in our lives as well.

Father, thank you for quenching my thirst with water and my thirsty soul with your presence. In Jesus' name. Amen.

AUGUST 28

Psalm 104:19-23

He made the moon to mark the seasons,
and the sun knows when to go down.
You bring darkness, it becomes night,
and all the beasts of the forest prowl.
The lions roar for their prey
and seek their food from God.
The sun rises, and they steal away;
they return and lie down in their dens.
Then people go out to their work,
to their labor until evening.

Note to Self: Praise the Lord Today!
(Continued)

Psalm 104 is a call to praise. In yesterday's portion of the psalm, water was used as an example of why we should praise God. The liquid we take for granted is essential to life. We wouldn't make it a week without it. Today the moon and sun are used for the same purpose – a call to praise the Lord.

The cycle of the day provides God's creation with all it needs. For people, the day provides a time for work and the evening a time for rest. For some animals, the evening is a time to search for food. For man and beast, the moon marks the seasons to enjoy the variety of the summer's heat and the winter's cold.

Since the sun rises and sets every day, just like clockwork, we can easily miss this great cycle that God provides. Today, praise God for his creation – the rising sun and the heat of "high noon." Praise him in the evening when you see the moon. Let it remind you of God's blessings throughout the day. God's blessings are all around us – even in the daily cycle that we take for granted. The psalmist calls us to open our eyes, watch for God and give him praise.

Father, thank you for the sun, moon and stars. Allow me to ponder your creation and give you praise for the great blessing of a daily cycle. Help me see your hand at work all around me. Help me to watch for you. In Jesus' name. Amen.

AUGUST 29

Psalm 104:24-30

*How many are your works, L*ORD*!*
> *In wisdom you made them all;*
> *the earth is full of your creatures.*

There is the sea, vast and spacious,
> *teeming with creatures beyond number –*
> *living things both large and small.*

There the ships go to and fro,
> *and Leviathan, which you formed to frolic there.*

All creatures look to you
> *to give them their food at the proper time.*

When you give it to them,
> *they gather it up;*

when you open your hand,
> *they are satisfied with good things.*

When you hide your face,
> *they are terrified;*

when you take away their breath,
> *they die and return to the dust.*

When you send your Spirit,
> *they are created,*
> *and you renew the face of the ground.*

Significant in Christ

Saving Private Ryan is an epic war film set during the invasion of Normandy in World War II. The film follows U.S. Army Ranger Captain John H. Miller (played by Tom Hanks) and his squad as they search for Private First Class James Francis Ryan, who is the last surviving brother of four servicemen. Miller loses several of his men in their search to find Ryan. After finding Ryan, Miller, himself, is mortally wounded. As he lay dying, he tells Ryan, "Earn this."

Years later, an old Private Ryan stands in front of Miller's grave and says, "Every day I think about what you said to me that day on the bridge. I tried to live my life the best that I could. I hope that was enough. I hope that, at least in your eyes, I've earned what all of you have done for me." Turning to his wife, an emotional Ryan says, "Tell me I have led a good life . . . Tell me I'm a good man."

The fear of insignificance comes in the form of an internal question: "Have I done enough with this one and only life that God has given me?" On our own we can never convince ourselves that we have, but things change with Jesus. He died for us so that we don't have to earn anything. By his grace we can live lives "satisfied with good things." Now the question becomes: "Is the work of Jesus enough to make me satisfied and significant?" The answer to that question is always, "Yes!"

Father, thank you for sending your Son to make me innocent and righteous in your sight. Thank you for making me significant. In Jesus' name. Amen.

AUGUST 30

Psalm 104:31-35

May the glory of the Lord endure forever;
> may the Lord rejoice in his works –

he who looks at the earth, and it trembles,
> who touches the mountains, and they smoke.

I will sing to the Lord all my life;
> I will sing praise to my God as long as I live.

May my meditation be pleasing to him,
> as I rejoice in the Lord.

But may sinners vanish from the earth
> and the wicked be no more.

Praise the Lord, my soul.

Praise the Lord.

Beyond the Last Note

You don't have to be an accomplished vocalist to sing praises to God. The believer is challenged to belt out proclamations of worship every day, all day, "as long as I live." Our tunes of praise may be personal renditions of well-known hymns or contemporary praise melodies, but "singing" is not the only way to "sing to the Lord."

A life song is proclaimed throughout God's daily assignments. Beautiful songs are sung when mothers tenderly care for their children and when fathers provide godly encouragement. Life songs hit the high notes when we serve others behind the scenes. Harmony is heard when believers work together in unity. Praise rocks as we choose obedience over disobedience when no one is watching. Forgiving one another is a song that brings tears of joy.

Singing praises to God in the gathering of other believers is essential, powerful and encouraging. It is the spiritual turbo charge that spurs our praise during the week. However, praise doesn't stop with the last note of the worship set. The most powerful praise songs are sung when you walk into your office or classroom on Monday morning with the attitude that proves you are a child of the living God.

Father, make my life a song of praise that honors you with worship as long as I live. In Jesus' name. Amen.

AUGUST 31

Psalm 105:1-11

Give praise to the Lord, proclaim his name;
> *make known among the nations what he has done.*

Sing to him, sing praise to him;
> *tell of all his wonderful acts.*

Glory in his holy name;
> *let the hearts of those who seek the Lord rejoice.*

Look to the Lord and his strength;
> *seek his face always.*

Remember the wonders he has done,
> *his miracles, and the judgments he pronounced,*

you his servants, the descendants of Abraham,
> *his chosen ones, the children of Jacob.*

He is the Lord our God;
> *his judgments are in all the earth.*

He remembers his covenant forever,
> *the promise he made, for a thousand generations,*

the covenant he made with Abraham,
> *the oath he swore to Isaac.*

He confirmed it to Jacob as a decree,
> *to Israel as an everlasting covenant:*

"To you I will give the land of Canaan
> *as the portion you will inherit."*

Practical Praise

Praise is both a spiritual and practical experience. It forms deep within the soul and comes forth in song or proclamation, and shows itself just as real in delivering a meal to a family in need. How can we make known to others what God has done? How can we practically tell of his wonderful acts? Here are some examples purposed to encourage you to practical praise.

- Visit a person in a nursing home. Read Scripture and pray with them.
- Take a meal to a person who is unable to come to church. Encourage them with the ministry of presence and God's Word.
- Shovel the snow from a neighbor's driveway or mow their grass when they're gone on vacation.
- Drive a person to his/her treatment. Stay with them during the procedure.
- Volunteer in a ministry of your church.
- Use your spiritual gift – up front or behind the scenes.

The spiritual experience of praise is significant, but so is the practical application. Practical praise demands that we break from our holy huddles and run some plays on the field of life. Practical praise will allow us to honor God through serving people and engaging in conversations about all God's wonderful acts.

Father, give me meaningful experiences of spiritual and practical praise. Help me see that down-to-earth application gives me great opportunities to tell of your wonderful deeds. In Jesus' name. Amen.

SEPTEMBER 1

Psalm 105:12-22

When they were but few in number,
    few indeed, and strangers in it,
they wandered from nation to nation,
    from one kingdom to another.
He allowed no one to oppress them;
    for their sake he rebuked kings:
"Do not touch my anointed ones;
    do my prophets no harm."

He called down famine on the land
    and destroyed all their supplies of food;
and he sent a man before them –
    Joseph, sold as a slave.
They bruised his feet with shackles,
    his neck was put in irons,
till what he foretold came to pass,
    till the word of the L<small>ORD</small> proved him true.
The king sent and released him,
    the ruler of peoples set him free.
He made him master of his household,
    ruler over all he possessed,
to instruct his princes as he pleased
    and teach his elders wisdom.

God Never Wastes Your Time

Whatever you are going through, you can be sure of this: God is not wasting your time. You may feel overlooked, sidelined, alone. God has not forgotten you. He is using your present pain to prepare you for his plan. Today's passage is a reminder of this truth.

When the nation of Israel was no more than a family clan, a severe famine threatened their survival. However, prior to the famine, God had so orchestrated events that one member of their family, Joseph, had been sold as a slave and then, through a series of God-ordained circumstances, was put in charge of Egypt's food supply. Joseph's family moved to Egypt and grew to be a strong nation. (This story is found in Genesis 37-50.)

It is encouraging to read the entire account of Joseph's life and see how God put all the pieces together. But, granted, going through the long days can challenge your faith. Pray that God will encourage you each day to trust him and be strengthened by him.

Father, I know you work all things out for good, but the pain of today makes me doubt that truth. I am tired and disheartened. I cannot imagine how today's pain will prepare me for tomorrow. But . . . I know you love me and I trust you. I trust you even through my doubt and discouragement. Help me to trust when I cannot understand. Help me to trust even when I cannot see an end to the pain. You sent your Son to die for my sins. I know you will give me everything I need for today. I pray in Jesus' name. Amen.

SEPTEMBER 2

Psalm 105:23-38

Then Israel entered Egypt;
    Jacob resided as a foreigner in the land of Ham.
The LORD made his people very fruitful;
    he made them too numerous for their foes,
whose hearts he turned to hate his people,
    to conspire against his servants.
He sent Moses his servant,
    and Aaron, whom he had chosen.
They performed his signs among them,
    his wonders in the land of Ham.
He sent darkness and made the land dark –
    for had they not rebelled against his words?
He turned their waters into blood,
    causing their fish to die.
Their land teemed with frogs,
    which went up into the bedrooms of their rulers.
He spoke, and there came swarms of flies,
    and gnats throughout their country.
He turned their rain into hail,
    with lightning throughout their land;
he struck down their vines and fig trees
    and shattered the trees of their country.
He spoke, and the locusts came,
    grasshoppers without number;
they ate up every green thing in their land,
    ate up the produce of their soil.
Then he struck down all the firstborn in their land,
    the firstfruits of all their manhood.
He brought out Israel, laden with silver and gold,
    and from among their tribes no one faltered.
Egypt was glad when they left,
    because dread of Israel had fallen on them.

God Never Wastes Our Time

Can you imagine a situation where God's great blessings turned things south? That's what happened to the nation of Israel. After moving to Egypt to escape death by famine, God blessed them and "made his people very fruitful." However, the growth became a threat and soon Israel lived under Egypt's oppression.

Today's passage recounts God's intervention. He sent Moses and Aaron to deliver his people from cruelty and tyranny. God demonstrated his power with a series of supernatural actions. Finally, Egypt relented and "was glad when they left, because dread of Israel had fallen on them."

The story of Israel's deliverance is a great reminder that we are never forsaken or forgotten. Our God is a God who sees. He never takes his eyes off those he loves. He is on your side. He is the great Deliverer. Keep praying. Keep waiting. Keep watching. God is on the way.

Father, thank you for being the great Deliverer. Help us to wait patiently and expectantly for you. In Jesus' name. Amen.

SEPTEMBER 3

Psalm 105:39-45

He spread out a cloud as a covering,
*   and a fire to give light at night.*
They asked, and he brought them quail;
*   he fed them well with the bread of heaven.*
He opened the rock, and water gushed out;
*   it flowed like a river in the desert.*

For he remembered his holy promise
*   given to his servant Abraham.*
He brought out his people with rejoicing,
*   his chosen ones with shouts of joy;*
he gave them the lands of the nations,
*   and they fell heir to what others had toiled for —*
that they might keep his precepts
*   and observe his laws.*

Praise the Lord.

Daily Deliverance

Our need for God's deliverance is never "one and done" or "two and through." Our thanksgiving for yesterday's relief quickly turns into a new prayer for another rescue. There is never a day when we are not depending on God.

After God delivered Israel from Egypt, the journey through the wilderness began. The nation needed God more than ever. They were free from Egypt, but not free from their need for God. They needed protection during the day. They needed light to guide them during the dark nights. They needed food. They needed water. Every day . . . God provided exactly what they needed.

And every day . . . God will provide exactly what you need. Let him know your needs today. Thank him for his provisions tonight. Thank God that he reminds you often of your dependence on him. If not, you might start thinking you were good to go on your own.

Father, keep me dependent on you. There I will always find all I need. In Jesus' name. Amen.

SEPTEMBER 4

Psalm 106:1-5

Praise the Lord.

Give thanks to the Lord,
    for he is good; his love endures forever.

Who can proclaim the mighty acts of the Lord
    or fully declare his praise?
Blessed are those who act justly,
    who always do what is right.

Remember me, Lord, when you show favor to your people,
    come to my aid when you save them,
that I may enjoy the prosperity of your chosen ones,
    that I may share in the joy of your nation
    and join your inheritance in giving praise.

His Love Endures Forever

Psalm 106 describes the "mighty acts" that God performed for his people. Even when the people of Israel turned their backs on God, he never turned his back on them. Our heavenly Father's love "endures forever."

Many times love is conditional. You may have had parents who demonstrated their love only when you performed well. They expressed great pride over good grades, touchdowns, homeruns, first chairs and lead roles. However, you felt their disappointment with B's or C's, fumbles, strikeouts or mediocre performances. The love of the heavenly Father is different. His love endures forever; and since it is a perfect love, it is free from conditions.

When I trust in the Lord and become a child of God, there is nothing I can do to make him love me more; there is nothing I can do to make him love me less. He will love me as much tomorrow as he does today. That does not give me a license to sin; rather, it inspires me to obey my Father whose love endures forever.

Thank you, Father, for your enduring love. Thank you for taking away my worries that you might withdraw your love based on my performance. Thank you for your perfect, unconditional, lasting love that is mine through Jesus. In his name I pray. Amen.

SEPTEMBER 5

Psalm 106:6-15

We have sinned, even as our ancestors did;
   we have done wrong and acted wickedly.
When our ancestors were in Egypt,
   they gave no thought to your miracles;
they did not remember your many kindnesses,
   and they rebelled by the sea, the Red Sea.
Yet he saved them for his name's sake,
   to make his mighty power known.
He rebuked the Red Sea, and it dried up;
   he led them through the depths as through a desert.
He saved them from the hand of the foe;
   from the hand of the enemy he redeemed them.
The waters covered their adversaries;
   not one of them survived.
Then they believed his promises
   and sang his praise.

But they soon forgot what he had done
   and did not wait for his plan to unfold.
In the desert they gave in to their craving;
   in the wilderness they put God to the test.
So he gave them what they asked for,
   but sent a wasting disease among them.

Wait for His Plan to Unfold

Psalm 106 describes God's work during a period in the history of Israel. He delivered them from Egypt, led them across the Red Sea, and was taking them to the Promised Land. However, they "soon forgot what he had done and did not wait for his plan to unfold."

It's easy to forget what God has done. Our days are filled with pressing needs and busy activities that swallow any time for reflection. "God, what have you done for me today?" unfortunately becomes our mantra.

Slow down. Reflect on what God has done. God's powerful activity not only delivers us from the present danger, but provides confidence that he is more than capable of delivering us tomorrow. Don't forget what God did yesterday. Wait on him today. Let his plan unfold for tomorrow.

Father, slow us down. Help us to reflect. Don't let us forget. You promise that the same power that saves us will provide us with everything we need. In Jesus' name. Amen.

SEPTEMBER 6

Psalm 106:16-23

In the camp they grew envious of Moses
      and of Aaron, who was consecrated to the Lord.
The earth opened up and swallowed Dathan;
      it buried the company of Abiram.
Fire blazed among their followers;
      a flame consumed the wicked.
At Horeb they made a calf
      and worshiped an idol cast from metal.
They exchanged their glorious God
      for an image of a bull, which eats grass.
They forgot the God who saved them,
      who had done great things in Egypt,
miracles in the land of Ham
      and awesome deeds by the Red Sea.
So he said he would destroy them –
      had not Moses, his chosen one,
stood in the breach before him
      to keep his wrath from destroying them.

Don't Forget!

Someone has said that we need to be reminded more than we need to be taught. That was certainly the case for the nation of Israel in the Old Testament. God had done great things for them, but they forgot. They ignored the God who had saved them and "exchanged their glorious God for an image of a bull." Unfortunately, we have the same short-term memory.

God has done great things in our lives. While we were still sinners, Jesus died for us. Jesus carried our sins in his body on the cross. He paid the penalty for our sins with his death. He endured the cross, "scorning its shame."

Certainly we are impressed with the drying up of the Red Sea. We are fascinated with the miracles in the Old and New Testaments. The greatest miracle of all, though, is the death, burial and resurrection of Jesus. I don't know what you are going through today. I don't know the challenges you face or the pain you are enduring, but don't forget the God who saved you. If he gave you the greatest gift – eternity! – he is more than capable of meeting the needs in your life.

Father, don't let me be a "what have you done for me lately" believer. I pray that my thanksgiving and praise are always rooted in the cross. Don't let me forget you. In Jesus' name. Amen.

SEPTEMBER 7

Psalm 106:24-33

Then they despised the pleasant land;
　　they did not believe his promise.
They grumbled in their tents
　　and did not obey the Lord.
So he swore to them with uplifted hand
　　that he would make them fall in the wilderness,
make their descendants fall among the nations
　　and scatter them throughout the lands.

They yoked themselves to the Baal of Peor
　　and ate sacrifices offered to lifeless gods;
they aroused the Lord's anger by their wicked deeds,
　　and a plague broke out among them.
But Phinehas stood up and intervened,
　　and the plague was checked.
This was credited to him as righteousness
　　for endless generations to come.
By the waters of Meribah they angered the Lord,
　　and trouble came to Moses because of them;
for they rebelled against the Spirit of God,
　　and rash words came from Moses' lips.

Think Before You Sin

Moses was fed up with Israel. He had been God's instrument in the plagues, deliverance from Egypt, Red Sea crossing and nourishment in the desert, but the people continued to grumble and "did not obey the Lord."

One of Israel's great grumblings took place by the waters of Meribah. Israel blamed Moses for leading them out of Egypt. They refused to believe God's promises and believed, instead, that God had taken them to the wilderness to die of thirst. God instructed Moses, "Speak to the rock before their eyes and it will pour out its water." However, Moses was so frustrated with the people that he struck the rock twice with his staff. This rash disobedience was very costly.

We thank God for his love and forgiveness. We thank God for his restoration. But we cannot blame our sin on others. We cannot forget that sin has consequences. Moses was forgiven, but because of his sin he was not allowed to lead the people into the Promised Land. This is a solemn reminder. Be aware of the consequences before you sin.

Father, help us to think before we sin. Help us realize the solemn truth regarding sin's consequences. In Jesus' name. Amen.

SEPTEMBER 8

Psalm 106:34-39

They did not destroy the peoples
> *as the Lord had commanded them,*
but they mingled with the nations
> *and adopted their customs.*
They worshiped their idols,
> *which became a snare to them.*
They sacrificed their sons
> *and their daughters to false gods.*
They shed innocent blood,
> *the blood of their sons and daughters,*
whom they sacrificed to the idols of Canaan,
> *and the land was desecrated by their blood.*
They defiled themselves by what they did;
> *by their deeds they prostituted themselves.*

Grieving God

Are you an influencer or are you being influenced? Are you a leader or are you being led? Are you making a statement for Christ in your world or is the world making its statement on you?

Israel owned the history of God's deliverance and his assurances for the future, but instead of standing for God they bowed to anti-God forces. They forgot God's promises and bought into the world's philosophy.

How about you? Are you standing strong for Christ in your school, office and neighborhood? Do you proclaim the message of Christ in your world or – be honest – are you living the world's message of materialism, position and identity? Thomas Watson well said, "The sins of the wicked anger God – but the sins of professing Christians grieve him." It's not a "happy Bible story" question, but one that needs to be asked nevertheless: Are you grieving God with your sins?

Father, search me and make known my heart. Show me if there is anything in my life that is grieving you. Then give me the courage and strength to change. In Jesus' name. Amen.

SEPTEMBER 9

Psalm 106:40-48

Therefore the Lord was angry with his people
    and abhorred his inheritance.
He gave them into the hands of the nations,
    and their foes ruled over them.
Their enemies oppressed them
    and subjected them to their power.
Many times he delivered them,
    but they were bent on rebellion
    and they wasted away in their sin.
Yet he took note of their distress
    when he heard their cry;
for their sake he remembered his covenant
    and out of his great love he relented.
He caused all who held them captive
    to show them mercy.

Save us, Lord our God,
    and gather us from the nations,
that we may give thanks to your holy name
    and glory in your praise.

Praise be to the Lord, the God of Israel,
    from everlasting to everlasting.

Let all the people say, "Amen!"

Praise the Lord.

Time to Come Home

Psalm 106 is a history of Israel's rebellion and the consequences of their sin. This psalm is a reminder that God always takes sin seriously. God delivered Israel many times but "they were bent on rebellion." They received the consequences for their actions.

Sin cannot be excused or explained away. It not only impacts us but also those around us. We must be as serious about sin as God is. The Apostle John tells us that "if we confess our sins, he is faithful and just and will forgive us our sins and purify us from all unrighteousness" (1 John 1:9).

Today you can know God's complete pardon. He waits to welcome you home and embrace you with grace. Whatever you have done, however long you have done it, regardless of how far you have wandered away, God is ready to forgive and restore. You need not clean yourself up before coming to him. You can't! God alone is the Cleanser. "Come now, let us settle the matter," says the Lord. "Though your sins are like scarlet, they shall be as white as snow; though they are red as crimson, they shall be like wool" (Isaiah 1:18). It's time to leave your sin and come home.

Father, show me the path home. Give me strength to make the journey back. Let me feel your embrace of grace. In Jesus' name. Amen.

SEPTEMBER 10

BOOK V

Psalm 107:1-9

Give thanks to the Lord, for he is good;
  his love endures forever.

Let the redeemed of the Lord tell their story –
  those he redeemed from the hand of the foe,
those he gathered from the lands,
  from east and west, from north and south.

Some wandered in desert wastelands,
  finding no way to a city where they could settle.
They were hungry and thirsty,
  and their lives ebbed away.
Then they cried out to the Lord in their trouble,
  and he delivered them from their distress.
He led them by a straight way
  to a city where they could settle.
Let them give thanks to the Lord for his unfailing love
  and his wonderful deeds for mankind,
for he satisfies the thirsty
  and fills the hungry with good things.

Tell Your Story

What stories do you tell? The great new restaurant you tried last weekend? The trips you took this past year? A new techno-gadget that has changed your life? A favorite recipe? There's nothing wrong with sharing these, but wouldn't you agree that the redeemed have a greater story to tell?

The psalmist challenges believers to tell their stories. To be "redeemed" means to be purchased from slavery. There was a day when sin had us shackled. Then Jesus came. He set us free! He satisfied our spiritual thirst! He filled our hungry souls "with good things."

Here's my challenge: As an application to this portion of the psalm, tell your story to someone God has placed in your life. Tell them about his unfailing love. Tell them how he has changed your life . . . forever. Tell the thirsty and the hungry that Jesus can satisfy their deepest needs. Who needs to hear that God's love endures forever? Tell them your story.

Father, bring a person into my path who needs to hear about you. Give me the courage to tell my story of how you redeemed me. In Jesus' name. Amen.

SEPTEMBER 11

Psalm 107:10-16

Some sat in darkness, in utter darkness,
　　prisoners suffering in iron chains,
because they rebelled against God's commands
　　and despised the plans of the Most High.
So he subjected them to bitter labor;
　　they stumbled, and there was no one to help.
*Then they cried to the L*ORD *in their trouble,*
　　and he saved them from their distress.
He brought them out of darkness, the utter darkness,
　　and broke away their chains.
*Let them give thanks to the L*ORD *for his unfailing love*
　　and his wonderful deeds for mankind,
for he breaks down gates of bronze
　　and cuts through bars of iron.

Prison Break

Israel's rebellion led them to rough places. They "despised the plans of the Most High" and suffered the consequences of their sin. They were put in chains and taken captive by foreign nations. Then they cried out to God and he saved them.

Maybe you are experiencing a rough place as a result of personal rebellion. You understand the darkness, suffering and chains that come from despising the plans of the Most High. Here's the good news: You don't have to stay in prison!

Cry out to God. He will reach down and save you from your distress. He can break down the gates and bars that entrap you. He can set you free and refresh your life. He can deliver you from the darkness of prison and put you on a path illuminated by his Word. Today is the day to cry out to the Lord!

Father, I acknowledge my guilt. I despised your plans and chose my own path – a path that led to darkness and prison. I am trapped in sin. Forgive me for my rebellion. Today I cry out to you to deliver me. Please break down the gates and bars and free me by your grace and unfailing love. In Jesus' name. Amen.

SEPTEMBER 12

Psalm 107:17-22

Some became fools through their rebellious ways
>*and suffered affliction because of their iniquities.*
They loathed all food
>*and drew near the gates of death.*
Then they cried to the Lord in their trouble,
>*and he saved them from their distress.*
He sent out his word and healed them;
>*he rescued them from the grave.*
Let them give thanks to the Lord for his unfailing love
>*and his wonderful deeds for mankind.*
Let them sacrifice thank offerings
>*and tell of his works with songs of joy.*

Unfailing Love

When you are broken . . .
> *Give thanks to the Lord for his unfailing love.*

When you have failed those you love . . .
> *Give thanks to the Lord for his unfailing love.*

When you fall to the same sin . . . again . . .
> *Give thanks to the Lord for his unfailing love.*

When you feel abandoned . . .
> *Give thanks to the Lord for his unfailing love.*

When you feel alone . . .
> *Give thanks to the Lord for his unfailing love.*

When fear takes over . . .
> *Give thanks to the Lord for his unfailing love.*

When you have lost your way . . .
> *Give thanks to the Lord for his unfailing love.*

When you have disappointed yourself . . .
> *Give thanks to the Lord for his unfailing love.*

Father, thank you for your constant love. Thank you for never failing me even though I so often fail you. In Jesus' name. Amen.

SEPTEMBER 13

Psalm 107:23-32

Some went out on the sea in ships;
> *they were merchants on the mighty waters.*

They saw the works of the Lord,
> *his wonderful deeds in the deep.*

For he spoke and stirred up a tempest
> *that lifted high the waves.*

They mounted up to the heavens and went down to the depths;
> *in their peril their courage melted away.*

They reeled and staggered like drunkards;
> *they were at their wits' end.*

Then they cried out to the Lord in their trouble,
> *and he brought them out of their distress.*

He stilled the storm to a whisper;
> *the waves of the sea were hushed.*

They were glad when it grew calm,
> *and he guided them to their desired haven.*

Let them give thanks to the Lord for his unfailing love
> *and his wonderful deeds for mankind.*

Let them exalt him in the assembly of the people
> *and praise him in the council of the elders.*

Storms

Storms. No one is excused. They kick up quickly, unexpectedly, powerfully. They smash against our lives with tornado-like force. We struggle to stand. Sometimes we fall.

Storms. No one is excused. They come in the form of illness; surgery; chemo; radiation; MRIs, PET scans; doctor visits; hospital stays; depression. We battle to keep going. Sometimes we feel we are at the end of our ropes.

Storms. No one is excused. Bright skies turn into dark nights. "I don't love you anymore." You never saw it coming – separation; tears; pleading; silence; custody battles; rejection; aloneness. The darkness of uncertainty is a scary place.

Storms. No one is excused. We cry out to the Lord, and he always comes. Not always to heal. Not always to restore. But he always comes. Sometimes he stills the storm to a whisper. Sometimes he comes to still our frightened hearts.

Lord Jesus, thank you for always coming when I cry out. Thank you for stilling my heart. Help me keep my eyes on you in the storm. In your name I pray. Amen.

SEPTEMBER 14

Psalm 107:33-38

He turned rivers into a desert,
>*flowing springs into thirsty ground,*
and fruitful land into a salt waste,
>*because of the wickedness of those who lived there.*
He turned the desert into pools of water
>*and the parched ground into flowing springs;*
there he brought the hungry to live,
>*and they founded a city where they could settle.*
They sowed fields and planted vineyards
>*that yielded a fruitful harvest;*
he blessed them, and their numbers greatly increased,
>*and he did not let their herds diminish.*

God in the Desert

The desert. Hot. Dry. Thirsty. Blistering heat during the day; cold at night. No place to rest. No place for protection. Exposed. Vulnerable. Miserable.

Have you ever walked through the desert . . . your personal one? Spiritual dryness. Pain during the day; anxiety during the night. A secret sin exposed. A character flaw uncovered. A thirsty soul. Only mirages of water.

The desert. The place where God shows up. He takes the dry stretches and brings refreshment with pools of water. He sees our thirsty souls and sends satisfying springs. He feeds our famished hearts. He brings us to places of rest. Don't despise the desert. God does his best work there.

Father, come to me in my desert place. Quench my thirst. Feed my soul. Drive away my spiritual dryness with your presence. Bring me to a place of rest. In Jesus' name. Amen.

SEPTEMBER 15

Psalm 107:39-43

Then their numbers decreased, and they were humbled
    by oppression, calamity and sorrow;
he who pours contempt on nobles
    made them wander in a trackless waste.
But he lifted the needy out of their affliction
    and increased their families like flocks.
The upright see and rejoice,
    but all the wicked shut their mouths.

Let the one who is wise heed these things
    and ponder the loving deeds of the Lord.

See and Rejoice

The work of the Lord is unmistakable. The land, sky and sea proclaim his person and his power – and then it gets personal. God meets us right where we are and takes us to the places he wants us to be. He lifts "the needy out of their affliction." He brings spiritual blessings.

Followers of God see his work and rejoice. They exalt the omniscient God for his intimate knowledge. They praise the eternal God for his intervention in time. They sing to the all-powerful God for his deliverance. They contemplate the depths of God's love.

Those who don't follow God are confused. They are book smart, but lack wisdom. They have no mental compartment for the supernatural. They have no place in their hearts for the divine. When the wicked see the works of God, they can only stand in silence.

Father, thank you for intervening in my life and allowing me to have a personal relationship with you. Thank you for your love for me today and forever. May I live a life of true joy as I see you at work around me. In Jesus' name. Amen.

SEPTEMBER 16

Psalm 108:1-5

A song. A psalm of David.

My heart, O God, is steadfast;
  I will sing and make music with all my soul.
Awake, harp and lyre!
  I will awaken the dawn.
*I will praise you, L*ORD*, among the nations;*
  I will sing of you among the peoples.
For great is your love, higher than the heavens;
  your faithfulness reaches to the skies.
Be exalted, O God, above the heavens;
  let your glory be over all the earth.

Higher Than the Heavens

The love of God is a subject we will never be able to fully grasp. It is "higher than the heavens." However, as we seek to comprehend as much as we can, A. W. Tozer's teaching is helpful. Here are some of the things he notes about God's love in his book *The Knowledge of the Holy*.

Love is an essential attribute of God. All of God's attributes, Tozer explains, are expressed fully and together. God never suspends one in order to express another. Since he is self-existent, his love has no beginning. Since he is eternal, his love has no end. Since he is infinite, his love has no limits. Since he is holy, his love is pure.

God's Word assures us that he desires to be our friend. Tozer says, "No man with a trace of humility would first think that he is a friend of God; but the idea did not originate with men." God himself said that Abraham was his friend and he desires the same friendship with us.

Love is an emotional identification. Tozer writes, "It is a strange and beautiful eccentricity of the free God that He has allowed His heart to be emotionally identified with men. Self-sufficient as He is, He wants our love and will not be satisfied till He gets it. Free as He is, He has let His heart be bound to us forever."

Love takes pleasure in its object. "The Lord," Tozer says, "takes peculiar pleasure in His saints . . . Christ in His atonement has removed the bar to the divine fellowship. Now in Christ all believing souls are objects of God's delight."

Heavenly Father, thank you for loving me. Thank you for my relationship with you through Jesus. Thank you for calling me your friend. In Jesus' name. Amen.

SEPTEMBER 17

Psalm 108:6-13

A song. A psalm of David.

Save us and help us with your right hand,
    that those you love may be delivered.
God has spoken from his sanctuary:
    "In triumph I will parcel out Shechem
    and measure off the Valley of Sukkoth.
Gilead is mine, Manasseh is mine;
    Ephraim is my helmet,
    Judah is my scepter.
Moab is my washbasin,
    on Edom I toss my sandal;
    over Philistia I shout in triumph."

Who will bring me to the fortified city?
    Who will lead me to Edom?
Is it not you, God, you who have rejected us
    and no longer go out with our armies?
Give us aid against the enemy,
    for human help is worthless.
With God we will gain the victory,
    and he will trample down our enemies.

The Enemy Crusher

Enemies. People who want to destroy. "Friends" who want to slander. Inappropriate Facebook posts. Unfitting Instagrams. Gossipers. Behind the backers. Things that destroy our person.

Enemies. Cancer. Chronic pain. Reoccurring illness. MS. Diabetes. ALS. Persistent fatigue. Addictions. Heart disease. Death. Things that destroy our bodies.

Enemies. Discouragement. Depression. Anxiety. Mood swings. Personality disorders. Panic. Things that destroy our emotions.

Enemies. We need help. Human help is ultimately worthless. We need supernatural aid. We need someone who can "gain the victory" on the field of battle. We need someone to stop the advance. We need someone who can demand retreat. We need someone to stand up and wield defeat. We need an enemy crusher.

Enemies. **We need God!**

Father, you are our only aid against the enemy. You are the only One who can gain the victory. You are the only One who can trample down our enemy. We need you. Please come to our aid. In Jesus' name. Amen.

SEPTEMBER 18

Psalm 109:1-5

For the director of music. Of David. A psalm.

My God, whom I praise,
>   do not remain silent,
for people who are wicked and deceitful
>   have opened their mouths against me;
>   they have spoken against me with lying tongues.
With words of hatred they surround me;
>   they attack me without cause.
In return for my friendship they accuse me,
>   but I am a man of prayer.
They repay me evil for good,
>   and hatred for my friendship.

Retreat to Pray

The proverb says, "Reckless words pierce like a sword" (Proverbs 12:18). Ever been pierced? Ever been run through? Ever been the subject of gossip or slander? Ever been verbally attacked without cause? Ever been the recipient of a social media slam? Ever had a friend turn on you? You are not alone.

David was going through a rough time of caustic criticism. His associates were fabricating lies about him. They were condemning him for no good reason. David felt that his expression of friendship had been returned with harsh allegations.

Notice David's response, "I am a man of prayer." David could not respond to every reckless word, but he could give all of his hurt, frustration and anger to God. What should be our response to unjust criticism? Charging to engage in verbal battle is not the answer. Retreating in prayer is. Let God devise the best plan of action and follow him in carrying it out.

Father, my knee-jerk reaction to criticism is to strike back. Forgive me. Help me retreat in prayer. Help me clearly hear the steps you want me to take. Help me to be a person of prayer. In Jesus' name. Amen.

SEPTEMBER 19

Psalm 109:6-15

For the director of music. Of David. A psalm.

Appoint someone evil to oppose my enemy;
> let an accuser stand at his right hand.
When he is tried, let him be found guilty,
> and may his prayers condemn him.
May his days be few;
> may another take his place of leadership.
May his children be fatherless
> and his wife a widow.
May his children be wandering beggars;
> may they be driven from their ruined homes.
May a creditor seize all he has;
> may strangers plunder the fruits of his labor.
May no one extend kindness to him
> or take pity on his fatherless children.
May his descendants be cut off,
> their names blotted out from the next generation.
May the iniquity of his fathers be remembered before the LORD;
> may the sin of his mother never be blotted out.
May their sins always remain before the LORD,
> that he may blot out their name from the earth.

Righteous Zeal

David was a champion of righteousness. He was the king of a theocracy – a nation ruled by God. He longed to see God's cause lived out on earth. In this psalm David recounts that a person had betrayed him. David's prayer for vindication was not personal. He desired that God judge the sin and stop the sinner from hurting others.

In the New Testament our prayer changes in light of God's full revelation. Jesus told us to pray for our enemies. We pray that he will change their hearts, and we also pray that God will stop wicked people from hurting others. From the imprecatory prayers of the psalms we are reminded that we should have a righteous zeal for God to be honored and his people protected.

Some questions to consider: Are you angered by those who oppose God? Are you praying that God will deal with terrorists who behead innocent people and persecute Christians? Does disobedience stir your heart? Are you calloused to hearing God's name taken in vain? Are you comfortable with wickedness . . . in your life and in the lives of others? Do you have a righteous zeal for God to be honored and his people protected?

Father, never let us be comfortable with sin. Create or renew in us a righteous zeal. As we pray for our enemies let us pray also that you are honored and your people protected. In Jesus' name. Amen.

SEPTEMBER 20

Psalm 109:16-25

For the director of music. Of David. A psalm.

For he never thought of doing a kindness,
> but hounded to death the poor
> and the needy and the brokenhearted.

He loved to pronounce a curse –
> may it come back on him.

He found no pleasure in blessing –
> may it be far from him.

He wore cursing as his garment;
> it entered into his body like water,
> into his bones like oil.

May it be like a cloak wrapped about him,
> like a belt tied forever around him.

May this be the Lord's payment to my accusers,
> to those who speak evil of me.

But you, Sovereign Lord,
> help me for your name's sake;
> out of the goodness of your love, deliver me.

For I am poor and needy,
> and my heart is wounded within me.

I fade away like an evening shadow;
> I am shaken off like a locust.

My knees give way from fasting;
> my body is thin and gaunt.

I am an object of scorn to my accusers;
> when they see me, they shake their heads.

A Wounded Heart

A wounded heart. Broken by a spouse. Bleeding from reckless words. Weighed down by rejection. Crying out for a prodigal. Shriveled by discouragement.

Have you ever experienced a wounded heart? David had. A person had betrayed him with rumors, gossip and slander. A onetime friend lashed out and tried to bring him down. The experience had left him weak, thin and gaunt. To those who believed the betrayer, David was an "object of scorn."

How should a wounded heart respond? For David, and us, there is only one thing to do – cry out to the "Sovereign Lord." Ask God to intervene. Pray for God's deliverance. He will come and initiate the healing process. Turn your wound over to God and let the recovery begin.

Father, I give my wounded heart to you. I turn myself over to your care and protection. I give myself to your sovereign recovery. In Jesus' name. Amen.

SEPTEMBER 21

Psalm 109:26-31

For the director of music. Of David. A psalm.

Help me, Lord my God;
> save me according to your unfailing love.

Let them know that it is your hand,
> that you, Lord, have done it.

While they curse, may you bless;
> may those who attack me be put to shame,
> but may your servant rejoice.

May my accusers be clothed with disgrace
> and wrapped in shame as in a cloak.

With my mouth I will greatly extol the Lord;
> in the great throng of worshipers I will praise him.

For he stands at the right hand of the needy,
> to save their lives from those who would condemn them.

Help Me!

Peter, the outspoken disciple, once saw Jesus walking on the water and wanted to do the same thing, so at Jesus' invitation he got out of the boat and started toward him. Then Peter realized what he was doing. He was struck with fear and began to sink. He cried out to Jesus, "Lord, save me." Jesus did.

Sometimes our prayers are filled with the poetry of the psalms. We thank God for his sovereign control and omnipotent hand in our lives. We thank him for the beauty of creation and for his blessings on our lives. Sometimes our prayers are like Peter's and the psalmist's. Due to fear, fatigue, anxiety, illness and/or confusion all we can pray is: "Help me, Lord my God, save me according to your unfailing love."

If that's where you are today I can promise you that God hears your cry for help. He knows exactly where you are and how you are feeling. He knows what is weighing down your soul and cluttering your mind. He knows that the storms of life can deliver doubt to the strongest heart. Just cry out, "Help me, Lord my God, save me . . . " He will.

Lord Jesus, I pray for the person who is exhausted. Just like you reached out and pulled Peter back into the boat, reach out and rescue the weary soul. Bring them to the safety of your presence. In your name I pray. Amen.

SEPTEMBER 22

Psalm 110

Of David. A psalm.

The Lord says to my lord:

"Sit at my right hand
 until I make your enemies
 a footstool for your feet."

The Lord will extend your mighty scepter from Zion, saying,
 "Rule in the midst of your enemies!"
Your troops will be willing
 on your day of battle.
Arrayed in holy splendor,
 your young men will come to you
 like dew from the morning's womb.

The Lord has sworn
 and will not change his mind:
"You are a priest forever,
 in the order of Melchizedek."

The Lord is at your right hand;
 he will crush kings on the day of his wrath.
He will judge the nations, heaping up the dead
 and crushing the rulers of the whole earth.
He will drink from a brook along the way,
 and so he will lift his head high.

Jesus Wins!

Today's psalm is the most direct prophecy about Jesus in the book of Psalms. It is called a "Messianic" psalm because it looks forward to the coming of the Messiah. Portions of this psalm are repeated by Jesus (Matthew 22:43-45; Mark 12:36-37; Luke 20:42-44), Peter (Acts 2:34-36), and the author of Hebrews (Hebrews 1:13; 5:6-10; 7:11-28). David wrote this as a great coronation song for the coming King.

Jesus' first coming did not look much like a coronation. His brief time on Earth was marred with rejection, challenge and, finally, death on a cross. However, this was all in God's plan. The great King came as our sacrifice so that we could one day live with him in his eternal kingdom.

One day at the name of Jesus every knee will bow and every tongue confess that he is the King of Kings and Lord of Lords. At the end of the day Jesus wins! He will reign forever and ever!

Lord Jesus, we acknowledge that you are the King of Kings and the Lord of Lords. May we live in surrender to your rule in our lives every moment of every day. In your name. Amen.

SEPTEMBER 23

Psalm 111:1-6

Praise the Lord. I will extol the Lord with all my heart
    in the council of the upright and in the assembly.

Great are the works of the Lord;
    they are pondered by all who delight in them.
Glorious and majestic are his deeds,
    and his righteousness endures forever.
He has caused his wonders to be remembered;
    the Lord is gracious and compassionate.
He provides food for those who fear him;
    he remembers his covenant forever.

He has shown his people the power of his works,
    giving them the lands of other nations.

Your Works are Glorious!

The word "ponder" means to "seek with care, consider something deeply and thoroughly, meditate upon." There are many of God's great works we could ponder, but for today let's consider one aspect of God's great creation – the stars.

Our sun, powerful enough to burn our skin and draw oxygen from every plant on earth, is a wimp among the stars. If the giant star Antares were positioned at the same location as the sun – 93 million miles away – Earth would be inside it! The sun and Antares represent just two of 500 billion stars that swim around the vast galaxy of the Milky Way! A dime held out at arm's length would block 15 million stars from view if our eyes could see with that power.

The galaxy Andromeda lies close enough (a mere two million light-years away) to see with the naked eye. It showed up on star charts long before the invention of the telescope. It is twice the size of the Milky Way and home to one trillion stars. Ready for this? The Milky Way and Andromeda are only two of one hundred billion galaxies all swimming with stars.

Tonight, take some time to go outside and look at the stars. Remember, the same God who set the stars sent his Son to die on the cross so you could be his son or daughter forever. Ponder that!

Father, all of your works are great. We are in awe of your power and your love that allows us to know you in a personal way. Slow us down to ponder your great works in the universe and in our lives. In Jesus' name. Amen.

SEPTEMBER 24

Psalm 111:7-10

The works of his hands are faithful and just;
　　all his precepts are trustworthy.
They are established for ever and ever,
　　enacted in faithfulness and uprightness.
He provided redemption for his people;
　　he ordained his covenant forever –
　　holy and awesome is his name.

The fear of the Lord is the beginning of wisdom;
　　all who follow his precepts have good understanding.
　　To him belongs eternal praise.

The Wisdom of Practical Obedience

Real wisdom is not found in an elite college classroom or the training center of a Fortune 500 company. True understanding does not come by devouring books or conducting ravenous research. Neither the blogger nor the consumer of blogs is necessarily prudent.

True wisdom begins when one action – *holy reverence* – is directed to one Person – *God*. Reverence is proven by practical obedience. Spurgeon wrote, "Men may know and be very orthodox, they may talk and be very eloquent, they may speculate and be very profound; but the best proof of their intelligence must be found in their actually doing the will of the Lord."

The answer to the question, "Are you a wise person?" is actually answered by a follow-up question, "Is your reverence proven by practical obedience?"

Father, make us truly wise. Give us hearts that truly honor and revere you. Give us hands that carry out worship in practical obedience. In Jesus' name. Amen.

SEPTEMBER 25

Psalm 112:1-5

Praise the Lord.

Blessed are those who fear the Lord,
    who find great delight in his commands.

Their children will be mighty in the land;
    the generation of the upright will be blessed.
Wealth and riches are in their houses,
    and their righteousness endures forever.
Even in darkness light dawns for the upright,
    for those who are gracious and compassionate
    and righteous.
Good will come to those who are generous and lend freely,
    who conduct their affairs with justice.

Blessing: The Ripple Effect

Today's passage is a great reminder for every parent and grandparent. Like a rock dropped in a pool of water, our actions ripple through the lives of our children and grandchildren.

The Lord blesses those who honor him. The investment of obedience today results in great dividends. That truth should give every parent and grandparent a solemn pause.

Take some time to let God drive that truth deep into your heart. Feel the weight of responsibility. My life cannot be about what delights me, but what brings pleasure to God. The person who finds great delight in God's commands today will pass on great blessing tomorrow.

Father, remind me often that my actions produce blessings or consequences. Help me find great delight in your commands. Move me past lip service to real action. In Jesus' name. Amen.

SEPTEMBER 26

Psalm 112:6-10

Surely the righteous will never be shaken;
> *they will be remembered forever.*
They will have no fear of bad news;
> *their hearts are steadfast, trusting in the Lord.*
Their hearts are secure, they will have no fear;
> *in the end they will look in triumph on their foes.*
They have freely scattered their gifts to the poor,
> *their righteousness endures forever;*
> *their horn will be lifted high in honor.*

The wicked will see and be vexed,
> *they will gnash their teeth and waste away;*
> *the longings of the wicked will come to nothing.*

Final Triumph

I was in the hospital room when the doctor arrived. The previous day's surgery revealed cancer. The doctor told my dad that the cancer was advanced and there was nothing that could be done. A nurse accompanied the doctor to give my dad a sedative after the news, but he didn't need it. He remained steadfast.

Many challenges followed that day until my dad went to be with the Lord five months later. I am sure my dad had the natural question of "Why?" and the sadness of leaving those he loved. I know some days the pain was unbearable for him. No doubt there were times of doubt and fear. However, I watched my dad die the way he had lived – trusting in the Lord.

The challenges of life hit hard. Uncertainty is the only certainty. A doctor's visit tomorrow, a phone call this afternoon can change everything. The true believer is not immune from fear, doubt, dread or discouragement. We feel pain and we grieve, but not like those who have no hope. We know with certainty in the end we will look in triumph over the final enemy. In Christ, death has been defeated. He leads us in victory from this life, through death, and into eternity.

Father, thank you for the steadfastness I have in Jesus. Thank you for the certain truth that one day I will pass from death to eternal life. Thank you for sending Jesus to blaze the path for me. I pray in his name. Amen.

SEPTEMBER 27

Psalm 113:1-3

Praise the Lord.

Praise the Lord, you his servants;
  praise the name of the Lord.
Let the name of the Lord be praised,
  both now and forevermore.
From the rising of the sun to the place where it sets,
  the name of the Lord is to be praised.

From the Rising of the Sun

Praise starts with the basics. Praise begins with those things that God gives to us each and every day. Praise continues as we watch for God's work around us from the rising to the setting of the sun. There is an old book called *The Valley of Vision* that contains a collection of Puritan prayers. Here is a prayer to remind us that everything around us provokes praise. Let this prayer be yours.

I thank thee for the temporal blessings of this world –
> *the refreshing air,*
> *the light of the sun,*
> *the food that renews strength,*
> *the raiment that clothes,*
> *the dwelling that shelters,*
> *the sleep that gives rest,*
> *the starry canopy of night,*
> *the summer breeze,*
> *the flowers' sweetness,*
> *the music of flowing streams,*
> *the happy endearments of family, kindred, friends.*

Things animate, things inanimate, minister to my comfort.
My cup runs over.
Suffer me not to be insensible to these daily mercies.
Thy hand bestows blessings: thy power averts evil.
I bring my tribute of thanks for spiritual graces,
> *the full warmth of faith,*
> *the cheering presence of thy Spirit,*
> *the strength of thy restraining will,*
> *thy spiking of hell's artillery.*

Blessed be my sovereign Lord!
> *– The Valley of Vision, p. 121*

SEPTEMBER 28

Psalm 113:4-9

The Lord is exalted over all the nations,
*   his glory above the heavens.*
Who is like the Lord our God,
*   the One who sits enthroned on high,*
who stoops down to look
*   on the heavens and the earth?*

He raises the poor from the dust
*   and lifts the needy from the ash heap;*
he seats them with princes,
*   with the princes of his people.*
He settles the childless woman in her home
*   as a happy mother of children.*

Praise the Lord.

He Stooped Down

Jesus left heaven to take on human flesh . . .
. . . the One who sits enthroned on high, who stoops down . . .

Born to a poor girl in a stable . . .
. . . the One who sits enthroned on high, who stoops down . . .

Although miraculously born he carried the stigma of illegitimacy . . .
. . . the One who sits enthroned on high, who stoops down . . .

He had no beauty to attract us to him . . .
. . . the One who sits enthroned on high, who stoops down . . .

He was despised and rejected by men . . .
. . . the One who sits enthroned on high, who stoops down . . .

He was a man of sorrows and familiar with suffering . . .
. . . the One who sits enthroned on high, who stoops down . . .

He was pierced for our transgressions . . .
. . . the One who sits enthroned on high, who stoops down . . .

He was crushed for our iniquities . . .
. . . the One who sits enthroned on high, who stoops down . . .

The punishment that gave us peace was on him . . .
. . . the One who sits enthroned on high, who stoops down . . .

By his wounds we are healed . . .
. . . the One who sits enthroned on high, who stoops down . . .

Lord Jesus, thank you for stooping down for us. Thank you for bearing our sin in your body on the cross. In your name. Amen.

SEPTEMBER 29

Psalm 114

When Israel came out of Egypt,
> *Jacob from a people of foreign tongue,*

Judah became God's sanctuary,
> *Israel his dominion.*

The sea looked and fled,
> *the Jordan turned back;*

the mountains leaped like rams,
> *the hills like lambs.*

Why was it, sea, that you fled?
> *Why, Jordan, did you turn back?*

Why, mountains, did you leap like rams,
> *you hills, like lambs?*

Tremble, earth, at the presence of the Lord,
> *at the presence of the God of Jacob,*

who turned the rock into a pool,
> *the hard rock into springs of water.*

Tremble in His Presence

This psalm is a hymn celebrating Israel's deliverance from slavery in Egypt. It was probably sung during Passover and other special times of worship. The psalmist asked the sea why it fled, the Jordan why it separated, and the mountains why they trembled. The answer: The Presence of God.

Today the presence of the same God of deliverance lives within our hearts. Just think about that! The all-powerful God lives within us in the form of the Holy Spirit. It is the Spirit that empowers us to live a life pleasing to God. By the Spirit we can say "No!" to sin and "Yes!" to obedience.

Are you experiencing that power? Are you experiencing the almighty God living in you and working through you? Are you surrendering to his empowerment or still trying to get it all done on your own? Maybe it's time we tremble at his presence and allow him to turn our hard hearts into springs of refreshing water.

Father, allow us to somehow grasp the fact that the power that caused the mountains to tremble is the same power we have through your Spirit. Help us give our lives over to the Spirit's control in order to know you intimately, love you passionately, and follow you wholeheartedly. In Jesus' name. Amen.

SEPTEMBER 30

Psalm 115:1-8

Not to us, Lord, not to us
> but to your name be the glory,
> because of your love and faithfulness.

Why do the nations say,
> "Where is their God?"
Our God is in heaven;
> he does whatever pleases him.
But their idols are silver and gold,
> made by human hands.
They have mouths, but cannot speak,
> eyes, but cannot see.
They have ears, but cannot hear,
> noses, but cannot smell.
They have hands, but cannot feel,
> feet, but cannot walk,
> nor can they utter a sound with their throats.
Those who make them will be like them,
> and so will all who trust in them.

Blurred Vision. Clear Trust.

At some point the prayer that comes from trembling lips and a shaken life is short and to the point – "I surrender." Jesus prayed fervently for the desires of his heart; yet submitted himself willingly to the sovereign plan of God. Like Jesus, we must submit ourselves to God's plan. God is sovereign; he "does whatever pleases him." But know this – everything that pleases him is good and right.

Back in 1676, a hymn writer named Samuel Rodigast had a dear friend who became seriously ill. In his fervent prayer for the friend's healing, Rodigast wrote these words:

> *Whate'er my God ordains is right:*
> *Holy His will abideth;*
> *I will be still whate'er He doth,*
> *And follow where he guideth:*
> *He is my God;*
> *Though dark my road,*
> *He holds me that I shall not fall:*
> *Wherefore to Him I leave it all.*
> *Whate'er my God ordains is right:*
> *He is my Friend and Father;*
> *He suffers naught to do me harm,*
> *Though many storms may gather,*
> *Now I may know both joy and woe,*
> *Someday I shall see clearly*
> *That He hath loved me dearly.*
> *Whate'er my God ordains is right:*
> *He never will deceive me;*
> *He leads me by the proper path,*
> *I know He will not leave me:*
> *I take, content,*
> *What He hath sent;*
> *His hand can turn my griefs away,*
> *And patiently I wait His day.*
> *Whate'er my God ordains is right:*
> *Here shall my stand be taken;*
> *Though sorrow, need, or death be mine,*
> *Yet I am not forsaken.*
> *My Father's care is round me there;*
> *He holds me that I shall not fall:*
> *And so to Him I leave it all.*

Father, to you I leave it all, knowing that someday I will see through all of life's challenges you have "loved me dearly." In Jesus' name. Amen.

OCTOBER 1

Psalm 115:9-13

All you Israelites, trust in the Lord –
he is their help and shield.
House of Aaron, trust in the Lord –
he is their help and shield.
You who fear him, trust in the Lord –
he is their help and shield.

The Lord remembers us and will bless us:
He will bless his people Israel,
he will bless the house of Aaron,
he will bless those who fear the Lord –
small and great alike.

Help and Shield

Israelite warriors went into battle with both offensive and defensive weapons. The spear allowed them to move forward and attack. The shield protected them against the enemy's armaments. Using the metaphor of war, the psalmist proclaimed God as the offensive weapon and defensive protection. He is our help and shield.

In his letter to the Ephesians, Paul takes this same analogy to the spiritual realm. Our battle is not against flesh and blood "but against the rulers, against the authorities, against the powers of this dark world and against the spiritual forces of evil in the heavenly realms." Paul exhorts us to put on the full armor of God.

Prepare for battle with the belt of truth, breastplate of righteousness, and feet fitted with the gospel of peace. Keep the shield of faith up to protect against the "flaming arrows of the evil one." Be prepared with the sword of the Spirit, "which is the word of God." From the physical battlefields of the Old Testament to the spiritual battles today, God is still our help and shield.

Father, we need your help. We cannot advance without you. We need you as our shield. We are vulnerable without you by our side. Thank you for your help and protection. In Jesus' name. Amen.

OCTOBER 2

Psalm 115:14-18

May the Lord cause you to flourish,
    both you and your children.
May you be blessed by the Lord,
    the Maker of heaven and earth.

The highest heavens belong to the Lord,
    but the earth he has given to mankind.
It is not the dead who praise the Lord,
    those who go down to the place of silence;
it is we who extol the Lord,
    both now and forevermore.

Praise the Lord.

Flourish

The Prosperity Gospel is a heretical teaching promising health and wealth to those who follow God. Some flavors of this errant theology guarantee that God will take whatever you give and return the amount fourfold or even tenfold. While the Prosperity Gospel is scripturally out of bounds, praying for God's blessing is right in line with God's Word. In today's passage the psalmist prays that God will cause you to flourish. Let's get practical and personal with this prayer.

Father, I pray that you will cause my marriage to flourish. Allow (name your spouse) and me to honor you with our commitment to each other.

Father, please cause my family to flourish (name your children/ grandchildren). Restore and heal broken relationships and estrangement. Develop them into men and women who will love and serve you.

Father, please bless those who are ill (name those struggling with illness). I pray that you will restore their health. Help their love for you flourish in this challenging time.

Father, please bless my job/business (name your place of employment or the business you own). Help me to be a man/woman of integrity in the workplace. Allow my reputation as a follower of Jesus to flourish.

Father, you are the Maker of heaven and earth. Please keep me close to you and cause my commitment to you to flourish until I see you face to face.

In Jesus' name. Amen.

OCTOBER 3

Psalm 116:1-6

I love the Lord for he heard my voice;
  he heard my cry for mercy.
Because he turned his ear to me,
  I will call on him as long as I live.

The cords of death entangled me,
  the anguish of the grave came over me;
  I was overcome by distress and sorrow.
Then I called on the name of the Lord:
  "Lord, save me!"

The Lord is gracious and righteous;
  our God is full of compassion.
The Lord protects the unwary;
  when I was brought low, he saved me.

Down to One Prayer

The psalmist lived in real life. The "cords of death entangled" him. He was overcome with the "anguish of the grave" and overwhelmed with "distress and sorrow." The psalmist was down to one prayer: "Lord, save me!"

How about you? Can you relate? Are you familiar with distress and sorrow? Do you feel like the entanglement of sin, a bad decision, or a health issue is dragging you down? Are you down to one prayer? "Lord, save me!"

God hears your every cry and he responds. He is gracious – he gives us what we don't deserve. He is righteous – everything he does is good and just. He is full of compassion – he comes with a heart full of mercy. God will hear you even if you are down to one prayer.

Lord, save me! In Jesus' name. Amen.

OCTOBER 4

Psalm 116:7-14

Return to your rest, my soul,
    for the Lord has been good to you.

For you, Lord, have delivered me from death,
    my eyes from tears,
    my feet from stumbling,
that I may walk before the Lord
    in the land of the living.

I trusted in the Lord when I said,
    "I am greatly afflicted";
in my alarm I said,
    "Everyone is a liar."

What shall I return to the Lord
    for all his goodness to me?
I will lift up the cup of salvation
    and call on the name of the Lord.
I will fulfill my vows to the Lord
    in the presence of all his people.

Need Rest?

It's a good day when we can say to ourselves, "Return to your rest." There are times when anxiety fills our hearts, when fear builds an impenetrable fortress in our souls. There are times when dread settles like a heavy fog, when suffering makes us feel that everyone is out to get us. Now it's time, my soul, to return to rest.

The Lord is the one who brings us back to our rest. His strength delivers us from the fear of the grave. His compassion dries our tears. God's protection keeps us from stumbling. He is the one who allows us to walk "in the land of the living."

Therefore, we counsel ourselves, "Return to your rest, my soul, for the Lord has been good" to me. He is my Strength-Giver, my Peace-Giver and my Protector-Provider. In him alone I can find real rest.

Father, thank you for giving me the strength I need to make it through today. Thank you for drying my tears and bringing me to a place of peace. Thank you for keeping my feet from stumbling. Thank you for rest. In Jesus' name. Amen.

OCTOBER 5

Psalm 116:15-19

Precious in the sight of the Lord
    is the death of his faithful servants.
Truly I am your servant, Lord;
    I serve you just as my mother did;
    you have freed me from my chains.

I will sacrifice a thank offering to you
    and call on the name of the Lord.
I will fulfill my vows to the Lord
    in the presence of all his people,
In the courts of the house of the Lord –
    in your midst, Jerusalem.

Praise the Lord.

Faithful Servants

Death is an unwelcome guest. We cringe at its arrival. But *precious in the sight of the Lord is the death of his faithful servants.*

Death is an untimely visitor. It always comes too soon. But *precious in the sight of the Lord is the death of his faithful servants.*

Death is an unwanted intruder. Even at the end of a long life we hang on. Still death barges in. But *precious in the sight of the Lord is the death of his faithful servants.*

Death always has its way. Sometimes arriving in a moment. Sometimes through a long illness. Sometimes through the process of aging. But *precious in the sight of the Lord is the death of his faithful servants.*

Death is the last enemy. There is no glamour in any part of its process. It is a thief coming to take away all we have known. But *precious in the sight of the Lord is the death of his faithful servants.*

For the believer death is only a transition. Because of Jesus we will pass from death to eternal life. That's why we can say: *Precious in the sight of the Lord is the death of his faithful servants.*

Lord Jesus, thank you for conquering death for us. Thank you for the promise that we will pass from death to life. In your name. Amen.

OCTOBER 6

Psalm 117

Praise the LORD, all you nations;
    extol him, all you peoples.
For great is his love toward us,
    and the faithfulness of the LORD endures forever.

Praise the LORD.

Bookends of Praise

"Praise the Lord" begins and ends this short psalm of praise. In between these bookends is the call to worship the Lord. The invitation is to all nations and all peoples. Two reasons are given for this appeal: God's great love and God's enduring faithfulness.

> **God's Great Love.** God's love is evident all around us. It is seen in the beautiful creation that provides all we need from oxygen to water to food. It is experienced through the people God places in our lives. However, the greatest act of God's love is seen in the person of Jesus. God loved us so much that he sent his Son to die as our substitute on the cross. C. S. Lewis well said, "Though our feelings come and go, God's love for us does not."

> **God's Enduring Faithfulness.** God's steadfastness never ceases. He never grows tired of loving us. He never forgets to send daily mercies (Lamentations 3:23). He gives us the nourishment we need – physically and spiritually. From him comes meaningful encouragement.

Take time today to praise the Lord. Regardless of your circumstance Jesus is the reason to spend time in prayerful thanksgiving. Bookend your day with "Praise the Lord."

Father, today I praise you for . . . (Tell God the things in your life that you praise him for doing and providing).

OCTOBER 7

Psalm 118:1-7

Give thanks to the L<small>ORD</small>, for he is good;
his love endures forever.

Let Israel say:
"His love endures forever."
Let the house of Aaron say:
"His love endures forever."
Let those who fear the L<small>ORD</small> say:
"His love endures forever."

When hard pressed, I cried to the L<small>ORD</small>;
he brought me into a spacious place.
The L<small>ORD</small> is with me; I will not be afraid.
What can mere mortals do to me?
The L<small>ORD</small> is with me; he is my helper.
I look in triumph on my enemies.

A Prayer for the "Hard Pressed"

God's presence is the game changer. Left to ourselves we are defenseless. There is no protection in sight, but the Lord is with us. He drives away fear. He is on our side giving us just what we need just when we need it.

Use the blanks to personalize the following prayer for someone in your life who is "hard pressed."

Heavenly Father,

Please be with _____. Help _____ to know that you are with him/her. Allow _____ to feel the warmth of your presence. Give _____ the assurance that you are on his/her side. Let _____ know that whatever is standing in his/her way is no match for you.

Take away dread and fear. Help _____ to cast all his/her anxiety on you. Give _____ the strength to heave it on you like a farmer throws a heavy sack of grain into the bed of his pickup truck. Remind him/her that you are the Defeater of every enemy, even the last enemy. Calm the beat of _____ heart.
Quiet _____ soul in your presence.

In Jesus' name. Amen.

OCTOBER 8

Psalm 118:8-14

It is better to take refuge in the Lord
>*than to trust in humans.*
It is better to take refuge in the Lord
>*than to trust in princes.*
All the nations surrounded me,
>*but in the name of the Lord I cut them down.*
They surrounded me on every side,
>*but in the name of the Lord I cut them down.*
They swarmed around me like bees,
>*but they were consumed as quickly as burning thorns;*
>*in the name of the Lord I cut them down.*
I was pushed back and about to fall,
>*but the Lord helped me.*
The Lord is my strength and my defense;
>*he has become my salvation.*

A Parent's Prayer

The musical *Annie* has a song called "It's The Hard-Knock Life." The orphans sing about an "empty belly, rotten smelly, full of sorrow, no tomorrow" hard-knock life. While few of us can identify with the plight of orphans, everyone can relate to the hard-knocks that come in some form or fashion. As parents it's hard for us to watch our children take those hard-knocks.

Here's a prayer to pray for our children and grandchildren through the inevitable hard-knocks of life.

Heavenly Father,

Life will come with its hard-knocks. Our children will be pushed back and pushed around by situations beyond their control. They will know what it means to stumble. Many times they will be about to fall, and most of the time I won't be there to catch them. But you will always be right by their side.

Father, be their strength against the influencing crowd. Be their help against life's inevitable challenges. Defend them against their strongest temptation in their weakest moments. Let them know that they are never alone. May this confession always be on their lips: "He has become my salvation."

In Jesus' name. Amen.

OCTOBER 9

Psalm 118:15-25

Shouts of joy and victory
    resound in the tents of the righteous:
"The Lord's right hand has done mighty things!
    The Lord's right hand is lifted high;
    the Lord's right hand has done mighty things!"
I will not die but live,
    and will proclaim what the Lord has done.
The Lord has chastened me severely,
    but he has not given me over to death.
Open for me the gates of the righteous;
    I will enter and give thanks to the Lord.
This is the gate of the Lord
    through which the righteous may enter.
I will give you thanks, for you answered me;
    you have become my salvation.

The stone the builders rejected
    has become the cornerstone;
the Lord has done this,
    and it is marvelous in our eyes.
The Lord has done it this very day;
    let us rejoice today and be glad.

Lord, save us!
    Lord, grant us success!

A Prayer for Our Children's Success

Today's psalm reminds us that it is the Lord who does "mighty things!" He is the One who has opened the "gates of righteousness." Although he was rejected and put to death, now he has become the "cornerstone" that holds our relationship with God together.

The psalmist ends this portion with a prayer for something we all want – success. However, sometimes God's view of victory looks a bit different than ours. Here's a prayer to pray for your children and grandchildren. Let's pray that God will grant them his success.

Father, I pray that you would grant your success to (say their names).

> *Give them success in the lessons of losing.*
> *Give them success in serving others.*
> *Give them success in befriending the lonely.*
> *Give them success in caring for the unfortunate.*
>
> *Give them success in choosing friends.*
> *Give them success in using time wisely.*
> *Give them success in reading your Word daily.*
> *Give them success in prayer.*
>
> *Give them success in the pain of failure.*
> *Give them success in the accolades of achievement.*
> *Give them success in obeying your Word.*
> *Give them success in repentance.*
>
> *Give them success at following hard after you.*
> *Give them success at using the gifts you've given them.*
> *Give them success in standing for you*
> *…even if it means standing alone.*
>
> *In Jesus' name. Amen.*

OCTOBER 10

Psalm 118:26-29

Blessed is he who comes in the name of the Lord.
 From the house of the Lord we bless you.
The Lord is God,
 and he has made his light shine on us.
With boughs in hand, join in the festal procession
 up to the horns of the altar.

You are my God, and I will praise you;
 you are my God, and I will exalt you.

Give thanks to the Lord, for he is good;
 his love endures forever.

A Parent's Prayer: God's Light

The light of the Lord! It reveals the path ahead and illumines our hearts. It lets us know when we are cruising on the right path and when we have taken a dangerous detour. We pray that God's light always shines on us. That's a great prayer to pray for our children and grandchildren, too.

Heavenly Father,
Thank you, God, for making your light shine on
    (children/grandchildren).
Shine your light on their hearts . . .
    let them see their sin and turn to you.
Shine your light on their paths . . .
    let them see the right road to travel.
Shine your light on their temptations . . .
    let them see the way to escape.
Shine your light on their weaknesses . . .
    show them their desperate need for you.
Shine your light on their failures . . . reveal the hard lessons.
Shine your light on their successes . . .
    let them see that you cause each one.
Shine your light on their education . . . let them find your calling.
Shine your light on their friendships . . . let them find iron-sharpeners.
Shine your light on their relationships . . .
    let them see the rewards of purity.
Shine your light on their marriages . . .
    let them love and honor their spouses.
Shine your light on their vocations . . .
    let them see how to minister at work.
Shine your light on their disappointments . . .
    let them see your encouragement.
Shine your light on their loneliness . . . let them see your presence.
Shine your light on their doubts . . . reveal that you can be trusted.
Shine your light on their sin . . . let them see the way back home.
Shine your light on their fear . . .
    let them find your strength and comfort.
Shine your light on their lives . . .
    let them always follow hard after you.
In Jesus' name. Amen.

Psalm 119: Introduction

Psalm 119 is organized alphabetically. Each paragraph includes eight verses. Each verse of the paragraph begins with the same Hebrew letter. Verses 1-8 begin with "aleph," the first letter of the Hebrew alphabet; verses 9-16 each begin with "Beth," the second letter of the Hebrew alphabet, and so on.

In his excellent commentary on the Psalms, Allen Ross explains that this psalm is a collection of prayers and meditations on the Word of God. He notes that Scripture is referred to by ten synonyms: "Law," "Word," "Saying," "Commandment," "Statutes," "Judgment," "Precepts," "Testimony," "Way," and "Path."

The psalmist spoke of God's Word as his "delight." He desired to obey and meditate on Scripture. He wrote that he wanted God's Word to "renew" and "preserve" him. In this psalm the writer also refers to himself as God's servant twelve times.

The above has been adapted from Allen Ross' commentary on the Psalms in The Bible Knowledge Commentary (Victor Books, Wheaton, Ill. 1985).

OCTOBER 11

Psalm 119:1-8

א *Aleph*

Blessed are those whose ways are blameless,
 who walk according to the law of the Lord.
Blessed are those who keep his statutes
 and seek him with all their heart –
they do no wrong
 but follow his ways.
You have laid down precepts
 that are to be fully obeyed.
Oh, that my ways were steadfast
 in obeying your decrees!
Then I would not be put to shame
 when I consider all your commands.
I will praise you with an upright heart
 as I learn your righteous laws.
I will obey your decrees;
 do not utterly forsake me.

Blessing Follows Obedience

Blessing always follows obedience. It may not be immediate. There may be a period of painful waiting. Obedience may be the hardest thing you've ever done. However, blessing always follows those "who walk according to the law of the Lord," "who keep his statutes," and who "seek him with all their heart."

Obedience is not a matter of convenience. God does not give us his Word like a waiter hands us a menu to pick what we like and ignore what we don't. God has put forth his "precepts that are to be fully obeyed." Each of us will have parts of God's instruction that are a delight for us to observe, and other parts we will struggle to follow until the day we die. Hear the psalmist's emotion as he sighs, "Oh, that my ways were steadfast in obeying your decrees! Then I would not be put to shame when I consider all your commands."

Today we start a journey through Psalm 119, a psalm that focuses on the Word of God. Let's begin by asking God to help us be obedient in all of God's teaching, not just the instruction we find easy to follow.

Father, as we begin this psalm show us where we are coming up short. Help us be steadfast in obeying your entire love letter to us. In Jesus' name. Amen.

OCTOBER 12

Psalm 119:9-10

ב *Beth*

How can a young person stay on the path of purity?
    By living according to your word.
I seek you with all my heart;
    do not let me stray from your commands.

Twelve Inches Down

As I write this, four fallen pastors come to mind. Their straying rippled through local congregations and made headline news. Each situation is a hard reminder that reading the Bible, studying the Bible, preaching sermons about the Bible, and writing books on the Bible is not enough. Head knowledge must be transformed into action.

The question in today's passage is an important one. How can a person, young or old, stay on the path of purity? The answer: Do what God's Word says to do. That's pretty straightforward. However, many men and women have taken a dangerous detour when they neglected to move the knowledge in their head twelve inches south to their heart.

Staying on the path begins with a promise and a plea. We must be committed to seeking God with all our hearts, minds, emotions and wills. We plead for God's desire and strength to never stray from his perfect instruction.

Father, never allow us to think another Bible study makes us a spiritual person. Keep driving the truth from our heads to our hearts. Never let us get comfortable with more knowledge without meaningful application. In Jesus' name. Amen.

OCTOBER 13

Psalm 119:11-16

ב *Beth*

I have hidden your word in my heart
    that I might not sin against you.
Praise be to you, Lord;
    teach me your decrees.
With my lips I recount
    all the laws that come from your mouth.
I rejoice in following your statutes
    as one rejoices in great riches.
I meditate on your precepts
    and consider your ways.
I delight in your decrees;
    I will not neglect your word.

Basic Instruction Before Leaving Earth

A man once came up to me in our church lobby and asked, "Do you know what the word "Bible" means?" My mind went to the Greek and the meaning of "biblios." I was getting ready to impress him with the original language when he said, "B-I-B-L-E. **B**asic **I**nstruction **B**efore **L**eaving **E**arth."

The Bible, God's love letter to us, gives the basic instructions for life and living. That's why the psalmist delighted in it and hid it in his heart. He memorized God's Word in order to guard against temptation and sin. He likened the privilege of knowing and following God's instruction to having great riches.

The world presents many attractive options. Temptation lures our hearts to pursue happiness. However, following temptation will always lead to places of destructive decisions, actions and habits. God's Word keeps us on his path. It provides us with basic instruction before we meet our Savior face to face.

Father, keep us in your Word. Keep our hearts delighted to read, study and apply your love letter to us. Help us memorize key verses. Help us to not neglect regular interaction with you. In Jesus' name. Amen.

OCTOBER 14

Psalm 119:17-24

ג *Gimel*

Be good to your servant while I live,
    that I may obey your word.
Open my eyes that I may see
    wonderful things in your law.
I am a stranger on earth;
    do not hide your commands from me.
My soul is consumed with longing
    for your laws at all times.
You rebuke the arrogant, who are accursed,
    those who stray from your commands.
Remove from me their scorn and contempt,
    for I keep your statutes.
Though rulers sit together and slander me,
    your servant will meditate on your decrees.
Your statutes are my delight;
    they are my counselors.

Eyes Wide Open

Quoting Isaiah, the Apostle Paul wrote, "'No eye has seen, no ear has heard, no mind has conceived what God has prepared for those who love him' – but God has revealed it to us by his Spirit" (1 Corinthians 2:9). God's Spirit knows God's thoughts; so when the believer reads God's Word it is the Spirit of God, living within us, who reveals God's words and thoughts to us.

Today's passage is a pre-Bible reading prayer. Our minds can be distracted. We can simply read the Bible to check off that day's reading from our "Read Through the Bible" guide. To help you focus, prior to reading God's Word I encourage you to pray the following prayer:

Heavenly Father,
Thank you for your Word, your love letter to me. Thank you for the privilege of opening it and reading it. I admit to you that I am in a hurry. I am busy and distracted, so please slow me down. Help me focus. Keep distractions away. Help me listen for things in your Word that I need to hear. Use your Word to point out areas of sin that I need to confess. Open my eyes to blind spots that I keep missing. Show me where I am off track. Open my eyes to a biblical perspective of where I am and where I should be. Instruct me regarding business interactions. Help me understand and apply your instructions that will guide my morning meetings. Instruct me regarding relationships. Open my eyes to hear from you regarding the person I am dating (if single) or my spouse (if married). I desire to be a godly parent. Open my eyes to see in your Word needed instruction that will help me raise my children. Lord, I desire to know you more fully and deeply. Speak to me in a new and fresh way through your Word. Father, please open my eyes to see your wonderful truths. In Jesus' name. Amen.

OCTOBER 15

Psalm 119:25-32

ד *Daleth*

I am laid low in the dust;
> preserve my life according to your word.

I gave an account of my ways and you answered me;
> teach me your decrees.

Cause me to understand the way of your precepts,
> that I may meditate on your wonderful deeds.

My soul is weary with sorrow;
> strengthen me according to your word.

Keep me from deceitful ways;
> be gracious to me and teach me your law.

I have chosen the way of faithfulness;
> I have set my heart on your laws.

I hold fast to your statutes, Lord;
> do not let me be put to shame.

I run in the path of your commands,
> for you have broadened my understanding.

Strength for the Weary Soul

Sorrow. It comes in many forms. The loss of health. The loss of a loved one. The death of a dream. Like a professional boxer it hits hard and then backs away only to strike again and again. It wears out body and soul.

There is one place to go for strength, a place that is living and active. A place where you can feel the inspired breath of God. A place of comfort. Peace. Reassurance. Security. Encouragement.

In times of sorrow open God's Word. Not to study, but to soak in his promises. Find a verse of comfort that washes over your soul and provides refreshment. Meditate on a passage that strengthens you deep within. When your soul is weary with sorrow find strength in God's Word.

Father, help me open your Word when I feel too weak, when sorrow has worn me down. Help me find an oasis of refreshment and strength. Give me encouragement through your Word. In Jesus' name. Amen.

OCTOBER 16

Psalm 119:33-40

ה He

Teach me, LORD, the way of your decrees,
> that I may follow it to the end.
Give me understanding, so that I may keep your law
> and obey it with all my heart.
Direct me in the path of your commands,
> for there I find delight.
Turn my heart toward your statutes
> and not toward selfish gain.
Turn my eyes away from worthless things;
> preserve my life according to your word.
Fulfill your promise to your servant,
> so that you may be feared.
Take away the disgrace I dread,
> for your laws are good.
How I long for your precepts!
> In your righteousness preserve my life.

Turn My Eyes From Worthless Things

The heart naturally beats for itself. It looks out for number one. We see life through customized lenses tinted with our desires, needs and personalities. Our view of life is evaluated by how it impacts us. That's why today's prayer is so important.

God's Word checks my heart. It shows me the right path. It calls me out when I take a detour. It shows me how to get on the road. It instructs me how to stay on the journey that God has for me.

There are many distractions that call out. They seem attractive from a distance; some are still attractive up close. However, these distractions are all off the road. They cause me to stop listening to God and feed my own desires. They turn my eyes toward worthless things. That's why I have to read God's Word regularly. It keeps me headed in a direction that honors God.

Father, please turn my heart to your Word. Please turn my eyes away from worthless things. Please preserve my life according to your Word. In Jesus' name. Amen.

OCTOBER 17

Psalm 119:41-48

ו *Waw*

May your unfailing love come to me, Lord,
> your salvation, according to your promise;
then I can answer anyone who taunts me,
> for I trust in your word.
Never take your word of truth from my mouth,
> for I have put my hope in your laws.
I will always obey your law,
> for ever and ever.
I will walk about in freedom,
> for I have sought out your precepts.
I will speak of your statutes before kings
> and will not be put to shame,
for I delight in your commands
> because I love them.
I reach out for your commands, which I love,
> that I may meditate on your decrees.

Where Is Your Trust?

What do you trust in? At the end of the day, what gives you confidence? What brings a sense of peace to your soul and allows you to sleep well at night?

Some answer those questions with financial security. They are certain that their investments will carry them through the rest of their lives. Others trust in their health. They exercise and eat well. Others put trust in people. A spouse or friend gives them needed stability. Still others place trust in national power. In a crazy world their confidence is in military might.

All the things mentioned above are good things. We should be wise with our money and connected with others. We should take care of our bodies. Who isn't for a strong military? However, each of these anchors of trust is vulnerable. God is the only One we can assuredly trust. God's unfailing love and the promises of his Word are the only certainties. Let us declare with the psalmist: "I trust in your word."

Father, thank you for your love that never disappoints. Thank you for your Word that never fails. Thank you for our provisions, families, friends and nation. Help us place our trust in you, not in people or things. In Jesus' name. Amen.

OCTOBER 18

Psalm 119:49-56

ז Zayin

Remember your word to your servant,
    for you have given me hope.
My comfort in my suffering is this:
    Your promise preserves my life.
The arrogant mock me unmercifully,
    but I do not turn from your law.
I remember, Lord, your ancient laws,
    and I find comfort in them.
Indignation grips me because of the wicked,
    who have forsaken your law.
Your decrees are the theme of my song
    wherever I lodge.
In the night, Lord, I remember your name,
    that I may keep your law.
This has been my practice:
    I obey your precepts.

Comfort in Suffering

James Stockdale was a U.S. Navy vice admiral and one of the most highly decorated officers in the history of the U.S. Navy. From September 9, 1968 until February 12, 1973, Stockdale was a prisoner of war in Vietnam.

Jim Collins interviewed Stockdale in his book *Good to Great*. Collins asked the Admiral how he survived the Vietnam POW camp. Stockdale said, "I never lost faith in the end of the story, I never doubted . . . that I would get out . . . You must never confuse faith that you will prevail in the end – which you can never afford to lose – with the discipline to confront the most brutal facts of your current reality, whatever they might be."

God's Word gives us hope – a certain confidence. It never gives us the option to give up. We will go through some difficult times, but even in the midst of our suffering, our comfort is in the fact that God's "promise preserves (our lives)." Regardless of what comes, we know that in the end, through Christ, we will prevail.

Father, keep me strong in my suffering. Help me never lose faith in the end of the story. My certain confidence is in knowing that whatever I experience in this life, I will spend eternity with you. Through Christ, I will prevail. Thank you in Jesus' name. Amen.

OCTOBER 19

Psalm 119:57-64

ח *Heth*

You are my portion, Lord;
> *I have promised to obey your words.*

I have sought your face with all my heart;
> *be gracious to me according to your promise.*

I have considered my ways
> *and have turned my steps to your statutes.*

I will hasten and not delay
> *to obey your commands.*

Though the wicked bind me with ropes,
> *I will not forget your law.*

At midnight I rise to give you thanks
> *for your righteous laws.*

I am a friend to all who fear you,
> *to all who follow your precepts.*

The earth is filled with your love, Lord;
> *teach me your decrees.*

A Re-Commitment Prayer

Lord, you are my portion. *I look to you to provide my every need and satisfy my deepest desire.*

I promise to obey your words. *I have experienced the failure of my own path. My commitment is to obey your instruction.*

I have sought your face with all my heart. *I will need your constant help. I know I am not capable of obedience on my own.*

Be gracious to me according to your promises. *I depend on your grace in my failure and your forgiveness for my restoration.*

I have considered my ways and have turned my steps to your statutes. *I ask that you examine my ways and turn my heart to know you more intimately, love you more passionately, and follow you wholeheartedly.*

In Jesus' name. Amen.

OCTOBER 20

Psalm 119:65-72

ט *Teth*

Do good to your servant
    according to your word, Lord.
Teach me knowledge and good judgment,
    for I trust your commands.
Before I was afflicted I went astray,
    but now I obey your word.
You are good, and what you do is good;
    teach me your decrees.
Though the arrogant have smeared me with lies,
    I keep your precepts with all my heart.
Their hearts are callous and unfeeling,
    but I delight in your law.
It was good for me to be afflicted
    so that I might learn your decrees.
The law from your mouth is more precious to me
    than thousands of pieces of silver and gold.

The Benefits of Affliction

Affliction. It comes in many forms. Illness. Slander. Rejection. Death. Discouragement. Job loss. Divorce. Prodigal child. Financial hit. The list goes on. Afflictions arrive uninvited and unwelcomed. Yet, when they come there are benefits.

The psalmist said, "It was good for me to be afflicted so that I might learn your decrees." Difficulties move us closer to God and his Word. They make us depend on him more deeply. They cause us to run to him for comfort. Challenging times highlight our hope.

In the midst of inevitable afflictions we turn to God for his sustaining grace. God is more real. His love is experienced more fully. Relationships are more cherished. The love for our spouses is deeper. Our children are held tighter. The sun shines brighter. The stars are more brilliant. The air is fresher. We can say with the psalmist, "It was good to be afflicted."

Father, in the midst of this storm I am clinging to you. Preserve me and protect me so that one day soon I can see your goodness in affliction. In Jesus' name. Amen.

OCTOBER 21

Psalm 119:73-80

י Yodh

Your hands made me and formed me;
> give me understanding to learn your commands.

May those who fear you rejoice when they see me,
> for I have put my hope in your word.

I know, Lord, that your laws are righteous,
> and that in faithfulness you have afflicted me.

May your unfailing love be my comfort,
> according to your promise to your servant.

Let your compassion come to me that I may live,
> for your law is my delight.

May the arrogant be put to shame for wronging me without cause;
> but I will meditate on your precepts.

May those who fear you turn to me,
> those who understand your statutes.

May I wholeheartedly follow your decrees,
> that I may not be put to shame.

Wholehearted

The world is full of choices. Food fills the shelves of the grocery store. Entire aisles are filled with candy to satisfy my sweet teeth (I have more than one). Cable television provides a menu of shows every hour of the day. There is no end to what I could watch. Smartphone apps bring choice to my fingertips. Within five minutes I can check social media, current news and the weather forecast. Cars. Investments. Insurance. Clothes. Travel. The world is filled with choices.

Sometimes the "Culture of Choice" follows me to God's Word. I like some commands, but not this one. This instruction seems reasonable, but not this one . . . at least not for today. I like this truth of theology, but this one is hard to grasp. Therefore, I choose what is most convenient and ignore the others. The "Culture of Choice" is a dangerous companion when considering God's Word.

Like the psalmist we must be people intent on following God's Word "wholeheartedly." We cannot pick and choose what sounds best at the moment. God does not include optional obedience in his love letter to us. All Scripture (not just some) is inspired by God. All Scripture is to be read, studied and applied. The "Culture of Choice" is no friend to God's holy instruction.

Father, like the psalmist, may I wholeheartedly follow your decrees, that I may not be put to shame. In Jesus' name. Amen.

OCTOBER 22

Psalm 119:81-88

כ *Kaph*

My soul faints with longing for your salvation,
  but I have put my hope in your word.
My eyes fail, looking for your promise;
  I say, "When will you comfort me?"
Though I am like a wineskin in the smoke,
  I do not forget your decrees.
How long must your servant wait?
  When will you punish my persecutors?
The arrogant dig pits to trap me,
  contrary to your law.
All your commands are trustworthy;
  help me, for I am being persecuted without cause.
They almost wiped me from the earth,
  but I have not forsaken your precepts.
In your unfailing love preserve my life,
  that I may obey the statutes of your mouth.

The Weariness of Waiting

Waiting . . . Waiting is one of the hardest exercises of the human soul. It invites "what if's," "when's" and "why's." It provides an open door to fear. It fills our hearts with rapid-fire thoughts that would seemingly fill the storage capacity of the iCloud. Anxiety feels like a stalker that hides in the darkness of our discouragement. Even when we can't "see" him, we can "feel" him.

The psalmist said that waiting did a number on his body. His "soul faints," his "eyes fail," and his mind has one big question, "When will you comfort me?" Maybe waiting is weighing you down today.

Lingering thoughts, consistent delays, persistent pain and unanswered questions drove the psalmist to one place: God's Word. When he felt like he was caught in a storm with no end in sight he threw down the anchor of God's promises. We must do the same thing. Use the weariness of waiting to cling to God's Word and his promises. His answers are always right on time.

Father, today I am waiting . . . for the pain to go away, for the doctor to call with test results, for a rebellious child to come home, for a spouse to return . . . Waiting is hard, but I trust in your Word and your promises. Please bring strength to my weary, waiting heart. In Jesus' name. Amen.

OCTOBER 23

Psalm 119:89-92

ל *Lamedh*

Your word, Lord, is eternal;
    it stands firm in the heavens.
Your faithfulness continues through all generations;
    you established the earth, and it endures.
Your laws endure to this day,
    for all things serve you.
If your law had not been my delight,
    I would have perished in my affliction.

The Consummate Constant

Change is the only constant. Tomorrow will never be the same as today.

- Friendships change. Think of the people you *used* to be close to.
- Children change. We blink and they are headed to college. How did that happen?
- Jobs change. According to the Bureau of Labor Statistics the average worker today stays at a job for just a little over four years.
- Technology changes. Remember life without a computer, Smartphone, iPad?
- Communities change. I can count 20 restaurants within two miles of my little corner of the world that have opened within the last five years.
- Appearance changes. Take a journey through Facebook on "Throw Back Thursday."
- Health changes. News flash: The human body is not built to live forever.
- Relationships change. Some husbands and wives grow closer while some drift apart.

There is one thing, however, that never changes. It is the consummate constant. God's Word stands firm forever. It is the never-changing truth in an ever-changing world. You can take hold of God's truth and never let go. The truth of God's Word will show you the path to eternal life.

Father, in the midst of constant change, thank you for your Word. It is the same yesterday, today and forever. Thank you for the sure anchor! In Jesus' name. Amen.

OCTOBER 24

Psalm 119:93-96

ל *Lamedh*

I will never forget your precepts,
>*for by them you have preserved my life.*
Save me, for I am yours;
>*I have sought out your precepts.*
The wicked are waiting to destroy me,
>*but I will ponder your statutes.*
To all perfection I see a limit,
>*but your commands are boundless.*

Life Preserver

Have you ever heard comments like these?

When I read the Bible in the morning, I have a great day. When I don't, my day doesn't go as well. – The "Good Luck Charm" Approach

I read the Bible for knowledge. – The "Textbook" Approach

I have a checklist to make sure I read the Bible every day. – The "To-Do List" Approach

I read an encouraging verse each morning. – The "Positive Thinking" Approach

Why do you read the Bible? Certainly there is nothing inherently wrong with knowledge, discipline or encouragement, unless . . . those things saturate your reasoning. God's Word is his love letter to you. It's from his heart to yours. It preserves you in a world intent on tearing you down and saves you in a world trying to drag you under.

Father, thank you for preserving me through your Word. In Jesus' name. Amen.

OCTOBER 25

Psalm 119:97-104

מ Mem

Oh, how I love your law!
    I meditate on it all day long.
Your commands are always with me
    and make me wiser than my enemies.
I have more insight than all my teachers,
    for I meditate on your statutes.
I have more understanding than the elders,
    for I obey your precepts.
I have kept my feet from every evil path
    so that I might obey your word.
I have not departed from your laws,
    for you yourself have taught me.
How sweet are your words to my taste,
    sweeter than honey to my mouth!
I gain understanding from your precepts;
    therefore I hate every wrong path.

Meditate

Do you ever watch those animal channels? The lions stalk the wildebeests or whatever and then all of a sudden the chase begins. The lion finally drags the thing down and kills it. Then lies in front of the animal and enjoys every nutritious morsel. That is a picture of the word "meditate." It is used to describe a lion enjoying his prey. He takes his time. Chews the food. Looks for every piece of meat. This is an instructive picture for reading God's Word.

You should read God's Word deliberately. Not in a hurry. Not just to check the daily reading box. Not just because your accountability partner is going to ask if you got your reading done. Not because the women in your study are keeping tabs. Not so you can tell your grandchildren you have read through the Bible every year since you were 35. The key word is: meditate.

Slow down and enjoy. Think on it for a while. "Chew" on it. Not just in your quiet time. Think it over on your way to work. Don't dismiss the truth when the day gets busy. Remember, this is good stuff. "Sweeter than honey." You're going to want to enjoy the feast all day long!

Father, help us savor your love letter to us. Help us meditate on it day and night. In Jesus' name. Amen.

OCTOBER 26

Psalm 119:105-106

נ *Nun*

Your word is a lamp for my feet,
   a light on my path.
I have taken an oath and confirmed it,
   that I will follow your righteous laws.

Changing Course

While on maneuvers, a battleship lookout spotted a light in the dark, foggy night. After noting the light's coordinates, the captain recognized his ship was on a collision course with another vessel. The captain instructed, "Signal the ship: We are on a collision course, advise you change course 20 degrees." The return signal countered, "Advisable for you to change course 20 degrees." The captain signaled, "I'm a captain, change course 20 degrees." The response was, "I'm a seaman second class, you'd better change course 20 degrees." By this time the captain was furious. His signal curtly ordered, "I'm a battleship. Change course 20 degrees." The reply: "I'm a lighthouse. You make the call." [1]

A lighthouse provides the light for the journey home. It directs those on the shifting sea away from danger and to a safe harbor. We must obey the direction provided by the light.

God's Word is the spiritual lighthouse that leads us through the journey of life and into eternity. It is a "lamp for my feet, a light on my path." It shows me the direction to go and keeps me from stumbling along the way. St. Augustine called the Bible, "Letters from home." God's Word comes from his heart and guides us to the eternal home he has prepared for us.

Father, guide us safely home by your Word. Help us see the path you provide and walk by your provision of light. In Jesus' name. Amen.

1 *The Seven Habits of Highly Effective People*, Stephen R. Covey, 1989, p. 32-33 (From Proceedings, magazine of the Naval Institute)

OCTOBER 27

Psalm 119:107-112

נ Nun

I have suffered much;
> preserve my life, Lord, *according to your word.*
Accept, Lord, *the willing praise of my mouth,*
> and teach me your laws.
Though I constantly take my life in my hands,
> I will not forget your law.
The wicked have set a snare for me,
> but I have not strayed from your precepts.
Your statutes are my heritage forever;
> they are the joy of my heart.
My heart is set on keeping your decrees
> to the very end.

My Inheritance

What will you inherit? A large sum of money? A family heirloom? A classic car? An estate? The family business? A new position? Many people live their lives waiting for that day when something of great value is handed down to them.

For the believer there is no need to wait! The psalmist says that God's Word is our great inheritance that we can enjoy forever. God's love letter is handed down to show us the way home and have a great time with him along the way.

God's Word teaches us the way to go, confronts us when we veer off the path, shows us how to get back on the path, and instructs us how to stay on the way that God has provided for us. With the psalmist we can say, "My heart is set on keeping your decrees to the very end."

Thank you, Father, for the rich inheritance of your Word. Help me keep your instruction until the last breath of my life. In Jesus' name. Amen.

OCTOBER 28

Psalm 119:113-120

ס *Samekh*

I hate double-minded people,
> but I love your law.

You are my refuge and my shield;
> I have put my hope in your word.

Away from me, you evildoers,
> that I may keep the commands of my God!

Sustain me, my God, according to your promise, and I will live;
> do not let my hopes be dashed.

Uphold me, and I will be delivered;
> I will always have regard for your decrees.

You reject all who stray from your decrees,
> for their delusions come to nothing.

All the wicked of the earth you discard like dross;
> therefore I love your statutes.

My flesh trembles in fear of you;
> I stand in awe of your laws.

Sustain Me

Sometimes the weight on our shoulders is burdensome. Our legs are heavy and our knees start to buckle. Dread fills our minds and acute anxiety takes our hearts hostage. During these times our prayer is a simple one – Lord, just keep me standing up.

The psalmist must have been going through a troublesome time when he prayed, "Sustain me, my God . . ." Help me withstand the challenge. Help me weather the storm. Support my body and soul. Allow me to endure. Protect me from the pressure. Don't "let my hopes be dashed."

Are you carrying a heavy burden today? Do you need God to uphold you? Are you afraid that your hopes will be dashed? Here is a prayer for you to take to the heavenly Father. He will hear and answer according to his promises.

Father, my heart is heavy. My body is worn down. My spirit is broken. My emotions are erratic. Disappointment in the past produces fear that my hopes will be dashed again. I can't stand the load any longer. I plead for you to uphold me. Please sustain me and I will praise you for your power and deliverance. Please support me today so I can praise you tomorrow. In Jesus' name. Amen.

OCTOBER 29

Psalm 119:121-128

ע *Ayin*

I have done what is righteous and just;
> do not leave me to my oppressors.

Ensure your servant's well-being;
> do not let the arrogant oppress me.

My eyes fail, looking for your salvation,
> looking for your righteous promise.

Deal with your servant according to your love
> and teach me your decrees.

I am your servant; give me discernment
> that I may understand your statutes.

It is time for you to act, Lord;
> your law is being broken.

Because I love your commands
> more than gold, more than pure gold,

and because I consider all your precepts right,
> I hate every wrong path.

Right and Almost Right

"Discernment," said C. H. Spurgeon, "is not a matter of simply telling the difference between right and wrong; rather it is telling the difference between right and almost right." Right and wrong are relatively easy to distinguish, but the difference between right and almost right needs special instruction from God's Spirit.

That's what the psalmist is praying for in today's psalm. He can see the bold colors of black and white; he needs help in the gray areas. He desires to understand the hard-to-see line that separates him from obedience and dangerous sin.

It takes only one bad lapse in judgment to ruin a reputation. An errant tweet, a foolish Facebook post, a regrettable Instagram picture, or a thoughtless text can bring down in a moment what has taken years to build. The psalmist's prayer is one for every serious believer: "I am your servant; give me discernment that I may understand your statutes."

Father, please give me discernment every moment of every day. Guard my responses, whether they come from my mouth or are posted on my smartphone. Give me discernment so that I can follow your Word in the areas that are right and almost right. In Jesus' name. Amen.

OCTOBER 30

Psalm 119:129-136

פ *Pe*

Your statutes are wonderful;
> therefore I obey them.

The unfolding of your words gives light;
> it gives understanding to the simple.

I open my mouth and pant,
> longing for your commands.

Turn to me and have mercy on me,
> as you always do to those who love your name.

Direct my footsteps according to your word;
> let no sin rule over me.

Redeem me from human oppression,
> that I may obey your precepts.

Make your face shine on your servant
> and teach me your decrees.

Streams of tears flow from my eyes,
> for your law is not obeyed.

Panting for God's Word

The psalmist reveals a solemn truth in today's passage – straying from God's Word is nothing but bad news. If God's instruction doesn't rule your life, sin will. The psalmist knows that when God's law is ignored sorrow is inevitable. He's been there and done that and doesn't want to be there and do that again.

Listen to the heart of the psalmist. He pants and longs for God's commandments. He wants to steer clear of sin. He desires redemption and obedience. He seeks God's smile of approval. He is full of shame when he misses the mark.

Isn't that the heart you want? Let's pray for that desire.

Father, help me approach your Word as the psalmist does in this passage. Remind me of my great need to hear from you daily. Remind me that my dark heart needs daily light. Remind me that my simple mind needs clear understanding. Remind me of my need for your mercy. Remind me that disobedience is a sad and sorrowful place. Please, Lord, make your face shine upon me and teach me your Word. In Jesus' name. Amen.

OCTOBER 31

Psalm 119:137-144

צ *Tsadhe*

You are righteous, Lord,
    and your laws are right.
The statutes you have laid down are righteous;
    they are fully trustworthy.
My zeal wears me out,
    for my enemies ignore your words.
Your promises have been thoroughly tested,
    and your servant loves them.
Though I am lowly and despised,
    I do not forget your precepts.
Your righteousness is everlasting
    and your law is true.
Trouble and distress have come upon me,
    but your commands give me delight.
Your statutes are always righteous;
    give me understanding that I may live.

Time Tested

Let's pray through our passage today.

Father, everything you do is right. You never make mistakes. Your judgment is pure. Everything you instruct me to do is right. I never have to second-guess your instruction. I know that following you will always keep me on a journey of obedience.

Lord, the saints throughout the years have thoroughly tested your Word. You have always been found trustworthy. "Your righteousness is everlasting and your law is true." I can put my full confidence in your Word. I know that you will never let me down.

There are times when trouble comes, when I feel "lowly and despised." I am no stranger to trouble and distress; but when I turn to your Word I find delight and understanding. In your Word there is comfort. In your Word there is confidence. Thank you for teaching me so that I may live.

In Jesus' name. Amen.

NOVEMBER 1

Psalm 119:145-152

ק *Qoph*

I call with all my heart;
> answer me, Lord, and I will obey your decrees.

I call out to you; save me
> and I will keep your statutes.

I rise before dawn and cry for help;
> I have put my hope in your word.

My eyes stay open through the watches of the night,
> that I may meditate on your promises.

Hear my voice in accordance with your love;
> preserve my life, Lord, according to your laws.

Those who devise wicked schemes are near,
> but they are far from your law.

Yet you are near, Lord,
> and all your commands are true.

Long ago I learned from your statutes
> that you established them to last forever.

God Is With You

There are times in our lives when we cry out to God for help. The people we thought we could trust have failed us. The things we put our hope in have faltered. We feel like we are going under. We need God to reach down and save us, to preserve our lives.

In this portion of Psalm 119 the psalmist felt the same way. He rose before the sun to let God know what was on his heart. "Those who devise wicked schemes" were near him. All day long he sought God. He reflected on God's promises – and he was not disappointed.

The psalmist discovered two things: God was with him and God's promises were true. People and things will disappoint us, but God's Word will never let us down. We know with certainty that God has established his Word to last forever. God will not disappoint us today, tomorrow or throughout eternity.

Father, it feels like I am going under. People oppose me. Circumstances discourage me. I feel alone. Remind me today that you are near. Guide me to the promises of your Word. Give me confidence in your eternal truth. In Jesus' name. Amen.

NOVEMBER 2

Psalm 119:153-160

ר *Resh*

Look on my suffering and deliver me,
> for I have not forgotten your law.

Defend my cause and redeem me;
> preserve my life according to your promise.

Salvation is far from the wicked,
> for they do not seek out your decrees.

Your compassion, Lord, is great;
> preserve my life according to your laws.

Many are the foes who persecute me,
> but I have not turned from your statutes.

I look on the faithless with loathing,
> for they do not obey your word.

See how I love your precepts;
> preserve my life, Lord, in accordance with your love.

All your words are true;
> all your righteous laws are eternal.

The Believer's "Go To"

Who do you call when your journey takes a sharp turn? Where do you go when unexpected circumstances barge in to your life? What do you do when you find some soft spots in what you thought to be solid? What's your "Go To" when discouragement and disappointment penetrate your soul?

The answer to these questions will vary. Some will have a good friend who is always a call and a cup of coffee away. Others will determine Christian counseling is needed to help clear the path of confusion. Still others will download a podcast and hear a needed message. All of these are valid and important sources, but I want to encourage you to make each of these your secondary source. Make God's Word your "Go To."

Scripture is God's love letter to you. Your heavenly Father wants to communicate his heart and give you his counsel. His compassion for you is incomparable. His words will preserve your life. Everything he says is true. All his words are right and eternal. Make God's Word your "Go To." Use his Word as the standard by which to evaluate all secondary sources.

Father, help me seek you first. Help me find guidance and encouragement in your Word. Help me make you my "Go To." Give me the discernment to evaluate all other sources according to your right and eternal Word. In Jesus' name. Amen.

NOVEMBER 3

Psalm 119:161-168

ש *Sin and Shin*

Rulers persecute me without cause,
> but my heart trembles at your word.

I rejoice in your promise
> like one who finds great spoil.

I hate and detest falsehood
> but I love your law.

Seven times a day I praise you
> for your righteous laws.

Great peace have those who love your law,
> and nothing can make them stumble.

I wait for your salvation, Lord,
> and I follow your commands.

I obey your statutes,
> for I love them greatly.

I obey your precepts and your statutes,
> for all my ways are known to you.

I Follow Your Commands

Billy Graham once said that if he had it to do all over again he would read less books about the Bible and spend more time reading the Bible itself. Books about the Bible are valuable. However, like Graham, we should desire to spend time in the primary source.

God's Word is not a textbook to be studied for a test, but a love letter to be absorbed for life. The psalmist tells us that his heart of calm comes from time in God's law. It warns of the obstacles on the journey so that nothing can make him stumble. Since God knows him inside and out, his precepts and statutes are relevant to his life. This desire for Scripture results in obedience. The psalmist says, "I obey your statutes, for I love them greatly."

Take your time in God's Word. Read a passage, then read it again. Ponder the Father's words just for you. Remember, all your ways are known to him. His eternal Word will speak directly to your heart.

Father, I don't want to treat the reading of your Word like a daily project. Help me read your Word as a love letter from my Father to his child. Help me see your commands as for my good. Help me hide your Word in my heart so that it will illuminate my path and keep me from taking dangerous detours. Thank you for your Word. In Jesus' name. Amen.

NOVEMBER 4

Psalm 119:169-176

ת *Taw*

May my cry come before you, Lord;
> give me understanding according to your word.

May my supplication come before you;
> deliver me according to your promise.

May my lips overflow with praise,
> for you teach me your decrees.

May my tongue sing of your word,
> for all your commands are righteous.

May your hand be ready to help me,
> for I have chosen your precepts.

I long for your salvation, Lord,
> and your law gives me delight.

Let me live that I may praise you,
> and may your laws sustain me.

I have strayed like a lost sheep.
> Seek your servant,
> for I have not forgotten your commands.

The Lost Are Found

Jesus once told a parable about a shepherd who had a hundred sheep. After making his daily count he discovered that one was missing. He left the ninety-nine and went after the lost sheep. When he found it he called his friends and neighbors and said, "Rejoice with me; I have found my lost sheep." Jesus said that the same rejoicing occurs in heaven when one sinner repents.

Today's psalm reminds us that sometimes we are that lost sheep. The Good Shepherd will always come searching. He will never give up on us. He will find us and bring us back home. He gives us the instruction to stay close to him.

That instruction is his Word, his love letter to us. The psalmist says, "your law gives me delight," "may your laws sustain me," and "I have not forgotten your commands." There is a way we can keep from straying – by living according to God's Word. The Good Shepherd provides his Good Word to keep us by his side.

Father, give me a hunger to desire your Word. I will always stray when I neglect your instruction. Help me stay close to you. Sustain me with your Word. In Jesus' name. Amen.

NOVEMBER 5

Psalm 120

A song of ascents.

I call on the Lord in my distress,
>and he answers me.
Save me, Lord,
>from lying lips
>and from deceitful tongues.

What will he do to you,
>and what more besides,
>you deceitful tongue?
He will punish you with a warrior's sharp arrows,
>with burning coals of the broom bush.

Woe to me that I dwell in Meshek,
>that I live among the tents of Kedar!
Too long have I lived
>among those who hate peace.
I am for peace;
>but when I speak, they are for war.

Before You Hit "Send"

Technology is a tremendous tool. I can use text messages to set up a meeting, share a passage of Scripture, or tell my kids how proud I am of them. Facebook can be used for ministry and communicating with friends. The same can be said about Twitter, Instagram, LinkedIn, Pinterest and Google+. These are great tools . . . and potential weapons. Words and pictures can be used to tear down a person and his or her reputation.

However, slander existed long before cyberspace. The desire to tear another person down started with Cain and Abel, and still exists today. As Old Testament believers made the climb to Jerusalem to celebrate the feasts, they prayed, "Save me, Lord, from lying lips and deceitful tongues."

Today's prayer is very instructive. We need to pray daily for God's protection from those who desire to destroy us by lies and deceit. We should also pray that God will protect us from sinful actions and foolish decisions that provide ammunition (like inappropriate social media postings). Jesus Christ is the message and we are the messengers. Let's pray that God will protect his messengers so that the Message is never confusing.

Father, we live in a day of great advantages and great dangers. Give us discernment with messages that go out on social media before we hit "send." Protect our interactions with the opposite sex. May our words and actions always be pure and above reproach. Help us to be messengers that are untainted so the message of your Son is never confused. In Jesus' name. Amen.

NOVEMBER 6

Psalm 121

A song of ascents.

I lift up my eyes to the mountains –
>   where does my help come from?
My help comes from the Lord,
>   the Maker of heaven and earth.

He will not let your foot slip –
>   he who watches over you will not slumber;
indeed, he who watches over Israel
>   will neither slumber nor sleep.

The Lord watches over you –
>   the Lord is your shade at your right hand;
the sun will not harm you by day,
>   nor the moon by night.

The Lord will keep you from all harm –
>   he will watch over your life;
the Lord will watch over your coming and going
>   both now and forevermore.

Maker of Heaven and Earth

The world is an uncertain place. Rogue nations continue to develop nuclear arms. Muslim extremists behead hostages and take over parts of the Middle East. Another virus breaks out and starts to show up around the world. Breaking news interrupts regularly scheduled programming to show viewers live footage of another natural disaster's aftermath.

Then it gets closer to home. Things change in our lives from day to day. Many have tests, treatments and surgeries that are on this week's schedule. Others have jobs that are on the bubble. Too many marriages are hanging together with one last thin thread of commitment. As you look to the mountainous challenges ahead, the words of the psalmist hit home, "Where does my help come from?"

The answer: The Lord! The Maker of heaven and earth! The unchanging God watches over you. He never sleeps, protecting you day and night. He leaves with you in the morning and comes home with you at night. He watches over you throughout the day. God is the only certainty. He will hold you with his unshakeable hand in your shaken world.

Father, help us hold on to you and never let go. Thank you for never letting go of us. In Jesus' name. Amen.

NOVEMBER 7

Psalm 122:1-5

A song of ascents. Of David.

I rejoiced with those who said to me,
> "Let us go to the house of the Lord."

Our feet are standing
> in your gates, Jerusalem.

Jerusalem is built like a city
> that is closely compacted together.

That is where the tribes go up –
> the tribes of the Lord –

to praise the name of the Lord
> according to the statute given to Israel.

There stand the thrones for judgment,
> the thrones of the house of David.

Celebrating God

Worshiping with other believers is a time of joy and celebration. The writer to the Hebrews reminds us not to neglect gathering times for the spiritual community. We come together to sing, praise, pray, hear God's Word and respond to what he is teaching us. When a person experiences real worship and says, "I got nothing out of it," that usually means they put nothing into it.

As Old Testament believers made their way to Jerusalem for the festivals, there was incredible expectation. It was a time of boundless rejoicing! There was no complaining about the crowds of people "closely compacted together." They were excited to be shoulder to shoulder with others who loved and worshiped God. More people, more worshipers – priceless!

How about you? Do you rejoice when it's time to gather for worship? Do you prepare yourself to meet with God? Are you joyful when people are "closely compacted together" in the worship center? Are you thrilled for your feet to be standing and praising God? Remember, worship starts with you. What you put into it is what you'll get out of it.

Father, the world is full of complainers, faultfinders and finger-pointers. Help us to be joyful worshipers and exultant servants of you – the Maker of heaven and earth. In Jesus' name. Amen.

NOVEMBER 8

Psalm 122:6-9

A song of ascents. Of David.

Pray for the peace of Jerusalem:
    "May those who love you be secure.
May there be peace within your walls
    and security within your citadels."
For the sake of my family and friends,
    I will say, "Peace be within you."
For the sake of the house of the L<small>ORD</small> *our God,*
    I will seek your prosperity.

Praying for Peace

Praying for peace. That is a significant call of Scripture. As believers we can certainly pray for the peace of Jerusalem. You need not agree with the action of Israel's present day government to believe that God has a special plan for his people. R. C. Sproul says, "I am persuaded that God will write a new chapter for ethnic Israel, for the Jewish people who are alive in the world today" (Now, That's a Good Question, p. 504).

So, "pray for the peace of Jerusalem," but don't stop there...

Pray for peace in the Middle East and for the protection of believers.
Pray for peace around the world and for the spread of the Gospel.
Pray for peace in the hearts of family members far from Jesus.
Pray for peace in the hearts of friends without Christ.
Pray for peace in families divided by stubborn selfishness.
Pray for peace in hearts interrupted by unwillingness to forgive.
Pray for peace in hearts infiltrated by sinful actions.
Pray for peace in homes challenged by different needs and personalities.
Pray for peace in marriages where confusion has taken hold.
Pray for peace in marriages where hurtful actions have left open wounds.
Pray for peace in churches threatened by disunity.
Pray for peace in minds that are pretentious and proud.
Pray for peace in emotions guided by irrational reasoning.
Pray for peace in attitudes of me-against-the-world.

Father, we pray for peace within our hearts. We seek your peace that passes all understanding. We desire a calmness that allows us to live and respond without regret. Father, we pray for peace . . . in our hearts . . . first. Let the peace you give us spread to those in our lives. In Jesus' name. Amen.

NOVEMBER 9

Psalm 123

A song of ascents.

I lift up my eyes to you,
> to you who sit enthroned in heaven.

As the eyes of slaves look to the hand of their master,
> as the eyes of a female slave look to the
> hand of her mistress,

so our eyes look to the LORD our God,
> till he shows us his mercy.

Have mercy on us, LORD, have mercy on us,
> for we have endured no end of contempt.

We have endured no end
> of ridicule from the arrogant,
> of contempt from the proud.

Have Mercy on Us

In grace God gives us what we don't deserve. It can't be bought with bags full of money. It cannot be earned with our best work performed over our best years. It can't be deserved by our best efforts on our best days. By grace God gives us what we don't deserve.

In mercy God doesn't give us what we do deserve. Our attitudes deserve a response. Our actions deserve punishment. Our opposition to God deserves his discipline. Our sin deserves his wrath. In his mercy God does not give us what we do deserve.

Our prayer is often that of the psalmist, "Have mercy on us, Lord, have mercy on us." We cannot claim innocence. We do not pronounce our purity. We stand before God in senseless sin. We plead with God to offer what we don't warrant – his mercy.

Father, have mercy on me. I admit my sin and sinfulness. I live in the contempt of my own construction. I come to you broken and repentant. I am thankful that you hold back what I deserve and give me what I don't deserve. Please continue to provide your grace and your mercy. In Jesus' name. Amen.

NOVEMBER 10

Psalm 124

A song of ascents. Of David.

If the Lord had not been on our side –
> let Israel say –
if the Lord had not been on our side
> when people attacked us,
they would have swallowed us alive
> when their anger flared against us;
the flood would have engulfed us,
> the torrent would have swept over us,
the raging waters
> would have swept us away.

Praise be to the Lord,
> who has not let us be torn by their teeth.
We have escaped like a bird
> from the fowler's snare;
the snare has been broken,
> and we have escaped.
Our help is in the name of the Lord,
> the Maker of heaven and earth.

Never Fight Alone

You do not want to fight the battle alone. The enemy is too strong, too powerful, too cunning and too evil. Go into the battle alone and you will be swallowed up, engulfed, swept over and swept away. You are not up for the fight. Go into combat alone and you will be defeated. Not "If," not "When?" but "For Sure!" Unless your help is in the name of the Lord, get ready for a shellacking.

The Israelite warrior never went into battle unaccompanied. Soldiers who had his back surrounded him, but he depended on more than other fighters. He went into battle with confidence when he knew that the Lord was on his side. It was the Lord alone who kept him from being torn apart by the enemies' weapons. It was the Lord alone who allowed him to escape.

How about you? It is not simply a lack of strategy, but a lack of sense to fight without the Lord. The battle belongs to him. The Maker of heaven and earth is more than capable of handling the enemy. The wise warrior, the winning warrior has this written on his heart: "My help is in the name of the Lord!"

Father, I will go into battle only if I can go with you. Without you I know the devastating outcome. I move out only with you by my side. Today I depend on you, my Help, my Protection, my Companion and my Friend. In Jesus' name. Amen.

NOVEMBER 11

Psalm 125

A song of ascents.

Those who trust in the Lord are like Mount Zion,
    which cannot be shaken but endures forever.
As the mountains surround Jerusalem,
    so the Lord surrounds his people
    both now and forevermore.

The scepter of the wicked will not remain
    over the land allotted to the righteous,
for then the righteous might use
    their hands to do evil.

Lord, do good to those who are good,
    to those who are upright in heart.
But those who turn to crooked ways
    the Lord will banish with the evildoers.

Peace be on Israel.

Surrounded

Jerusalem, the city that David captured from the Jebusites and later expanded, was built on two hills – Mount Zion on the west and the Ophel ridge on the east. Built on these hills the city stood secure. Mountains also surrounded Jerusalem and provided a powerful picture of how God encircled and protected his people.

Those who trust in the Lord experience the same confidence and defense. Our lives are built on the spiritual footing that God provided through his Son. Jesus, called Immanuel ("God with us") encompasses us with his person and his power.

The old hymn reminds us that our "hope is built on nothing less than Jesus' blood and righteousness." Our certain hope is built on the work and the Word of God. The Apostle Paul reminds us, "God's solid foundation stands firm, sealed with the inscription: 'the Lord knows those who are his'" (2 Timothy 2:19).

Father, thank you for making me yours through Jesus. Thank you for surrounding and protecting me like the mountains around Jerusalem. Thank you for the certainty of eternal life. Thank you for never leaving or forsaking me. Thank you for building my life on Jesus. In his name I pray. Amen.

NOVEMBER 12

Psalm 126

A song of ascents.

When the Lord restored the fortunes of Zion,
> we were like those who dreamed.
Our mouths were filled with laughter,
> our tongues with songs of joy.
Then it was said among the nations,
> "The Lord has done great things for them."
The Lord has done great things for us,
> and we are filled with joy.

Restore our fortunes, Lord,
> like streams in the Negev.
Those who sow with tears
> will reap with songs of joy.
Those who go out weeping,
> carrying seed to sow,
will return with songs of joy,
> carrying sheaves with them.

Laughter and Joy

The Israelites had been in the darkness of exile. They were taken captive and forcibly settled in another country. They dreamed of returning to Jerusalem and worshiping God together again in the community celebrations. Finally, under Ezra and Nehemiah, some were able to return. It is thought that this psalm was written for those who returned.

Those returning had to pinch themselves. They felt like they were in a dream. They could not contain their joy. It poured forth in laughter and songs of praise. They knew that the Lord had caused the return and the surrounding nations agreed, "The Lord has done great things for them."

Prior to life with Jesus we were in spiritual exile. You probably didn't experience captivity. In fact, you had surrounded yourself with some pretty nice stuff. However, your heart was imprisoned by spiritual darkness. Then Jesus came and opened your eyes. You saw your need for him and trusted in his work for you. Now you can say, "The Lord has done great things for me." Don't get over what Jesus did for you. Don't forget the laughter and the joy.

Father, thank you for sending Jesus to proclaim to me the Good News, to bind my broken heart, to set this captive free, and to bring me out of the darkness of spiritual confinement. Help me never get over the joy of my salvation. In Jesus' name. Amen.

NOVEMBER 13

Psalm 127

A song of ascents. Of Solomon.

Unless the Lord builds the house,
 the builders labor in vain.
Unless the Lord watches over the city,
 the guards stand watch in vain.
In vain you rise early
 and stay up late,
toiling for food to eat –
 for he grants sleep to those he loves.

Children are a heritage from the Lord,
 offspring a reward from him.
Like arrows in the hands of a warrior
 are children born in one's youth.
Blessed is the man
 whose quiver is full of them.
They will not be put to shame
 when they contend with their opponents in court.

Eternal Truth Into Tender Hearts

Parenting has always been challenging. Just consider these mothers from the past. Columbus' mother: "I don't care what you discovered, you still could have written!" Michelangelo's mother: "Can't you paint on walls like other children? Do you have any idea how hard it is to get that stuff off the ceiling?" Paul Revere's mother: "I don't care where you think you have to go, young man, midnight is past your curfew!" Albert Einstein's mother: "But it's your senior picture. Can't you do something about your hair?" And you thought you had it hard!

Children are a gift from God . . . even in the most challenging times. What you teach your children will stay with them always. What you fail to teach can be learned from no one else. You can build into little minds and hearts an understanding of unconditional love, tender care, and a belief system that will provide direction for life.

I know that your life is filled with exhausting chores and countless distractions. However, in the midst of it all don't miss the privilege of being with your children and taking advantage of those God-given teachable moments. God has given you the responsibility and privilege to implant eternal truth in a tender heart.

Father, give strength to the mom exhausted by early mornings, late nights and interruptions to her sleep. Give perspective to the dad working hard to make ends meet and trying to make the needed time for his family. Remind parents how fast the time goes and help them take advantage of every opportunity to implant your truth in a tender heart. In Jesus' name. Amen.

NOVEMBER 14

Psalm 128

A song of ascents.

Blessed are all who fear the Lord,
> *who walk in obedience to him.*

You will eat the fruit of your labor;
> *blessings and prosperity will be yours.*

Your wife will be like a fruitful vine
> *within your house;*

your children will be like olive shoots
> *around your table.*

Yes, this will be the blessing
> *for the man who fears the Lord.*

May the Lord bless you from Zion;
> *may you see the prosperity of Jerusalem*

all the days of your life.

May you live to see your children's children –
> *peace be on Israel.*

Blessed to Give

Fearing God is not a cowering terror. It is not all talk and no action. It does not hide secret sin behind a pretense of godliness. The fear of God is an awe and respect that honors God with one's whole life. The fear of God is, in one word: Obedience.

The Prosperity Gospel, taught by many, purports that God provides health and wealth in return for a cursory and conditional acknowledgment of him. This acknowledgment is often defined with money. It erroneously promises that God is beholden to bless me when I give to him. This psalm, however, teaches the truth about obedience.

Far from Prosperity Gospel, the psalmist declares the general truth of doing what God says – blessing follows obedience. Here God's blessings are found in the warmth and satisfaction of marriage and family. God blesses us so that we can pour ourselves into lives that will love God and continue to proclaim Christ in future generations. God doesn't bless us to get; he blesses us to give.

Father, continue to teach me that true blessing is giving myself away by loving and serving others in your name. Help me to never be selfish with my blessings or expectant with my obedience. In Jesus' name. Amen.

NOVEMBER 15

Psalm 129

A song of ascents.

"They have greatly oppressed me from my youth,"
    let Israel say;
"they have greatly oppressed me from my youth,
    but they have not gained the victory over me.
Plowmen have plowed my back
    and made their furrows long.
But the Lord is righteous;
    he has cut me free from the cords of the wicked."

May all who hate Zion
    be turned back in shame.
May they be like grass on the roof,
    which withers before it can grow;
a reaper cannot fill his hands with it,
    nor one who gathers fill his arms.
May those who pass by not say to them,
    "The blessing of the Lord be on you;
    we bless you in the name of the Lord."

Victory Is Mine

You may be oppressed, but you're not defeated. OK, so you're down, but you are not out. You may be on the short end of the score, but the game is far from over. Get your head up! Look up! The Lord does what is right and he will cut you free from the cords that bind you.

The psalmist was experiencing a tough time. From early in his life he was weighed down by heavy burdens. He describes the pain of his life as a plow digging a long furrow right down the middle of his back. However, even when others were greatly oppressing him he proclaimed, "but they have not gained the victory over me."

The enemy cannot and will not defeat you. He is incapable of gaining victory over you. Remember the words of Paul, "In all [of life's challenges] we are more than conquerors through him who loved us" (Romans 8:37). "Nothing in all creation can separate us from the love of God that is in Christ Jesus our Lord" (Romans 8:39). Death itself has been "swallowed up in victory" (1 Corinthians 15:54). Proclaim the truth with Paul and make it personal: "Thanks be to God! He gives [me] victory through [my] Lord Jesus Christ" (1 Corinthians 15:57).

Father, thank you for the final victory that you have promised me because of Jesus. Even when it feels like my back is being plowed, thank you that nothing in this life can gain victory over me. In Jesus' name. Amen.

NOVEMBER 16

Psalm 130:1-4

A song of ascents.

Out of the depths I cry to you, Lord;
　　Lord, hear my voice.
Let your ears be attentive
　　to my cry for mercy.

If you, Lord, kept a record of sins,
　　Lord, who could stand?
But with you there is forgiveness,
　　so that we can, with reverence, serve you.

Forgiveness: Costly and Free

Forgiveness. The word is powerful and tender, cleansing and costly. If God would keep a database of our sins we would be bowled over by indefensible and mounting guilt; but (say it out loud) **with God there is forgiveness!**

Here's what forgiveness looks like.

> *God removes our sins from us as far as the east is from the west.* — Psalm 103:12

> *God washes our hearts until they are as white as snow.* — Isaiah 1:18

> *God sweeps our sins away like a cloud.* — Isaiah 44:22

> *God hurls our sins into the depths of the sea.* — Micah 7:19

> *God paid the penalty of sin by sacrificing himself.* — Hebrews 9:26

> *Jesus "bore our sins" in his body on the cross.* — 1 Peter 2:24

> *He was pierced for our transgressions, he was crushed for our iniquities; the punishment that brought us peace was on him, and by his wounds we are healed.* — Isaiah 53:5

Father, thank you for your great sacrifice that purchased my forgiveness. May I never cease to thank you. In Jesus' name. Amen.

NOVEMBER 17

Psalm 130:5-8

A song of ascents.

I wait for the Lord, my whole being waits,
      and in his word I put my hope.
I wait for the Lord
      more than watchmen wait for the morning,
      more than watchmen wait for the morning.

Israel, put your hope in the Lord,
      for with the Lord is unfailing love
      and with him is full redemption.
He himself will redeem Israel
      from all their sins.

The Work of Waiting

Fast computers. Faster smartphones. Immediate results. Speed dating. Speed dialing. Microwaves. Drive-thru's. HOV Lanes. Most everything is built for speed – or we want it to be. We hate standing in lines, sitting in traffic jams and walking through security. Wait time is wasted time.

We bring the same expectations to God. We want him to answer our prayers right now. We want things cleared up by the next test. We want our first job to be the dream job. We want spiritual maturity in a fast five sessions. We want patience . . . and we want it NOW! We want microwave maturity.

God isn't on our clock, however. We have to wait for him . . . with our whole being. Like a watchman guarding his portion of the wall, so we stand at attention with all of our senses alert. We watch and watch and wait. It's in the waiting that we are stretched, which causes us to grow. We seek him and seek his Word. Time belongs to God. He is never late; he is seldom early. His timing is perfect – and he grows us in the waiting.

Father, I am waiting and I am tired of waiting. I feel like the watchman worn down and worn out from watching with all my being. Stretch me, grow me, embrace me as I wait for you. In Jesus' name. Amen.

NOVEMBER 18

Psalm 131

A song of ascents. Of David.

My heart is not proud, Lord,
> my eyes are not haughty;

I do not concern myself with great matters
> or things too wonderful for me.

But I have calmed and quieted myself,
> I am like a weaned child with its mother;
> like a weaned child I am content.

Israel, put your hope in the Lord
> both now and forevermore.

Counterfeit Holiness

Andrew Murray wrote, "The greatest test of whether the holiness we profess to seek or to attain is truth and life will be whether it produces an increasing humility in us. In man, humility is the one thing needed to allow God's holiness to dwell in him and shine through him. The chief mark of counterfeit holiness is lack of humility. The holiest will be the humblest."

Long before Murray, the psalmist pointed out the need for real humility. He desired to live with a humble heart. He wanted to keep his dreams and desires in check. He wanted to be like a "weaned" child walking by his mother with complete trust and contentment.

Like the mother who nursed her child, so God has provided us with everything we need. Now as we grow up we can walk beside him with confidence that he will give us what is best for us. Humility comes from a calm and quiet heart focused on God alone.

Father, keep pride far from my heart. Don't let me slow my growth by a lack of humility. Don't let me live with counterfeit holiness. Grow me stronger with increasing humility. In Jesus' name. Amen.

NOVEMBER 19

Psalm 132:1-5

A song of ascents.

Lord, remember David
 and all his self-denial.

He swore an oath to the Lord,
 he made a vow to the Mighty One of Jacob:
"I will not enter my house
 or go to my bed,
I will allow no sleep to my eyes
 or slumber to my eyelids,
till I find a place for the Lord,
 a dwelling for the Mighty One of Jacob."

Self-Denial

Self-denial. Without context the word sounds old, even legalistic. Self-fulfillment, self-satisfaction, self-esteem . . . now those are positive and encouraging words. Many want to do with more, not do without.

The psalmist calls the reader to "remember David and all his self-denial." The king longed to have a place for the Ark of the Covenant. While he was not the one who eventually built that dwelling place, he desired it for God. David was willing to do without to make God's name famous in his day.

Self-denial is an essential part of life. I can't eat everything I want to eat anytime I want to eat it and remain healthy. I can't focus so much on comfort that I refuse to exercise my body. I can't feed my sinful desires and develop as a follower of Jesus Christ. Are you willing to deny yourself what you want in order to get what you need?

Father, the world is full of unhealthy, out-of-shape, spiritually soft people who want more from you instead of more of you. May I be willing to deny myself what I want in order to get what I need. In Jesus' name. Amen.

NOVEMBER 20

Psalm 132:6-12

A song of ascents.

We heard it in Ephrathah,
> we came upon it in the fields of Jaar:
"Let us go to his dwelling place,
> let us worship at his footstool, saying,
'Arise, Lord, and come to your resting place,
> you and the ark of your might.
May your priests be clothed with your righteousness;
> may your faithful people sing for joy.'"

For the sake of your servant David,
> do not reject your anointed one.

The Lord swore an oath to David,
> a sure oath he will not revoke:
"One of your own descendants
> I will place on your throne.
If your sons keep my covenant
> and the statutes I teach them,
then their sons will sit
> on your throne for ever and ever."

Real Rest

Where do you find rest? What do you do to refresh your mind and body? For some, rest is found in a long afternoon nap on the weekends. For others, working out in the yard brings renewal. Some recuperate with a ride on their Harley, or on a boat out on the lake, or a hike in the mountains. Here's the follow-up question: Where do you find spiritual rest?

The Ark of the Covenant was the physical dwelling place of God on earth. It was his "footstool." It was called the ark of God's might because it was a symbol of his strength, power and victory in battle. The ark resided in Ephrathah (an old name for Bethlehem), then in Jaar for 20 years. Finally, David moved the ark to Jerusalem. The ark gave the Israelites confidence that God was with them. When the ark was near, they could rest.

Now, back to the question – Where do you find spiritual rest? As a believer, God now dwells in you by his Holy Spirit. We don't have to go to the temple or even to a church to meet God. Right now, right where you are you can find rest, confidence and strength. You need not depend on a symbol. The very presence of the living God is with you. Refresh your soul in him.

Father, I am tired. I need rest. Comfort me, refresh me, renew me and encourage me by your Spirit. I pray in Christ's name. Amen.

NOVEMBER 21

Psalm 132:13-18

A song of ascents.

For the LORD has chosen Zion,
> he has desired it for his dwelling, saying,
"This is my resting place for ever and ever;
> here I will sit enthroned, for I have desired it.
I will bless her with abundant provisions;
> her poor I will satisfy with food.
I will clothe her priests with salvation,
> and her faithful people will ever sing for joy.

"Here I will make a horn grow for David
> and set up a lamp for my anointed one.
I will clothe his enemies with shame,
> but his head will be adorned with a radiant crown."

Praise

The Lord chose Zion (Jerusalem) for his dwelling place. In that beautiful city the temple was built and the ark was placed. The ark symbolized God's presence and the temple was the place for worship. Believers gathered to worship in Jerusalem for the three annual feasts. During their captivity they longed to return there.

In the New Testament God moved his resting place from a physical structure to the heart of every person who trusts in Jesus for forgiveness of sins. Now he blesses us with abundant provisions and every spiritual blessing. He satisfies us with food that nourishes our souls. He clothes us with salvation.

When the Old Testament believers came together in Jerusalem there was great joy. They celebrated God's mercy and his faithfulness. They marveled at his grace. They basked in the overwhelming realization of his love. Today we need not travel to a "holy place" to experience the goodness of God. Right now, right where you are, thank God for everything he has done and is doing for you. He has chosen you for his dwelling place!

Father, thank you for choosing me for your dwelling place! Thank you for your great provisions. Thank you for all your spiritual blessings. Lord, help me to be a great giver of thanks. In Jesus' name. Amen.

NOVEMBER 22

Psalm 133

A song of ascents. Of David.

*How good and pleasant it is
       when God's people live together in unity!*

*It is like precious oil poured on the head,
       running down on the beard,
running down on Aaron's beard,
       down on the collar of his robe.
It is as if the dew of Hermon
       were falling on Mount Zion.
For there the Lord bestows his blessing,
       even life forevermore.*

The Power of Unity

Unity. It's a powerful word. It's an even more powerful experience. When families live in harmony life is good. Encouragement is rich when friends get along. When a team is moving in the same direction at the same time for the same reasons some great things are going to happen.

Today's psalm paints a vivid picture of unity. First, David describes anointing oil running down the priest's head, shoulders, and onto his breastplate with the names of the twelve tribes. The oil covering the tribes was a distinctive picture of unity. Second, David likened unity to the heavy dew on Mt. Hermon, symbolizing a nourishing and energizing flow of fresh water.

God placed us on this earth to do together what we could never do alone. We need each other to accomplish the things God put us on this earth to do. Let's move forward . . . together.

Father, help me live in unity as far as it depends on me. Help me to forgive others, encourage others, and move on from past hurts. Help me move forward in the strength of unity. In Jesus' name. Amen.

NOVEMBER 23

Psalm 134

A song of ascents.

Praise the Lord, all you servants of the Lord
    who minister by night in the house of the Lord.
Lift up your hands in the sanctuary
    and praise the Lord.

May the Lord bless you from Zion,
    he who is the Maker of heaven and earth.

Singing and Showing Our Praise

The Old Testament worshipers made their way up to Jerusalem for three annual feasts. As they traveled together they laughed, talked and sang. Their songs of ascents proclaimed love for God, love for one another and pure praise to the Maker of heaven and earth.

The worshipers couldn't wait for worship. They were ready to sing and show admiration for the living God. They anticipated lifting their hands in the sanctuary to actively demonstrate that God was worthy of their honor, awe and appreciation.

What about you? Do you anticipate worship with excitement? Do you prepare yourself before you arrive? Are you in place on time? Do you sing and show your admiration for God? God is worthy of all your praise! Sing it and show it!

Father, forgive me for hands-in-my-pockets worship. Forgive me for settling in halfway through the second song, distracting all those around me. Forgive me for being so easily sidetracked by my preferences and critiques. Help me praise you from the bottom of my heart. In Jesus' name. Amen.

NOVEMBER 24

Psalm 135:1-7

Praise the LORD.

Praise the name of the LORD;
> *praise him, you servants of the LORD,*
you who minister in the house of the LORD,
in the courts of the house of our God.

Praise the LORD, for the LORD is good;
> *sing praise to his name, for that is pleasant.*
For the LORD has chosen Jacob to be his own,
> *Israel to be his treasured possession.*

I know that the LORD is great,
that our Lord is greater than all gods.
The LORD does whatever pleases him,
> *in the heavens and on the earth,*
> *in the seas and all their depths.*
He makes clouds rise from the ends of the earth;
> *he sends lightning with the rain*
> *and brings out the wind from his storehouses.*

A Hallelujah Life

Anyone want to take a wild guess at what the psalmist is driving at in these verses? I am pretty sure the point is: Praise the Lord! The English phrase "Praise the Lord" comes from one powerful Hebrew word "Hallelujah." According to this psalm (and many passages like it), followers of the Lord are to live a "Hallelujah" life.

Praise is the act of expressing approval, admiration and adoration. It includes belting out songs from the tops of our lungs and the bottoms of our hearts, but it doesn't stop there. Praise must be expressed with all of our being. Some questions to consider:

- *Are you praising the Lord with your mouth?* Do your words truly demonstrate your admiration of the eternal God?
- *Are you praising the Lord with your mind?* Do your thoughts reflect his glory?
- *Are you praising the Lord with your actions?* Do you demonstrate a wholehearted love for God?
- *Are you praising the Lord with your money?* Does your virtual wallet demonstrate an expression of your commitment to serve him and others?

A "Hallelujah" life means more than just singing along with your favorite praise song downloads. Praise him with all you've got. He is worth far more than all you have.

Father, help us to live whole and complete hallelujah lives. In Jesus' name. Amen.

NOVEMBER 25

Psalm 135:8-14

He struck down the firstborn of Egypt,
> *the firstborn of people and animals.*

He sent his signs and wonders into your midst, Egypt,
> *against Pharaoh and all his servants.*

He struck down many nations
> *and killed mighty kings –*

Sihon king of the Amorites,
> *Og king of Bashan,*
> *and all the kings of Canaan –*

and he gave their land as an inheritance,
> *an inheritance to his people Israel.*

Your name, Lord, endures forever,
> *your renown, Lord, through all generations.*

For the Lord will vindicate his people
> *and have compassion on his servants.*

Proof for Faith

How can you know that God will take care of you today? How can you move into the unknown future with confidence? The writer to the Hebrews says that "faith is being sure of what we hope for and certain of what we do not see" (Hebrews 11:1). But how? How can you be so sure and so certain?

The answer to these questions is found in today's psalm. Israel saw the power of God in the plagues against Egypt. They watched God strike down nations and kill mighty kings. They inherited a land that God gave them. God proved himself to Israel over and over again. He does the same for us.

Trust is not blind. Present confidence is grounded in God's past work. God has demonstrated his might and power. Our trust is built on solid evidence. Like Israel, we believe God today because of what he accomplished yesterday. The road of faith is built with the bricks of God's past work.

Father, when my anxious heart starts to beat fast, slow it down with reminders of your past work in my life. When panic threatens today, turn it away with the work you accomplished in my life yesterday. Thank you for the proof that allows me to trust. In Jesus' name. Amen.

NOVEMBER 26

Psalm 135:15-21

The idols of the nations are silver and gold,
made by human hands.
They have mouths, but cannot speak,
eyes, but cannot see.
They have ears, but cannot hear,
nor is there breath in their mouths.
Those who make them will be like them,
and so will all who trust in them.

All you Israelites, praise the Lord;
house of Aaron, praise the Lord;
house of Levi, praise the Lord;
you who fear him, praise the Lord.
Praise be to the Lord from Zion,
to him who dwells in Jerusalem.

Praise the Lord.

Idols

Idols. Structures that stand tall but can't move an inch. Carved mouths are speechless. Chiseled eyes are sightless. Molded ears hear no sound. They are inanimate . . . lifeless . . . dead. People bow before their own creations.

Why do people bow before them? Why the burning incense? What's up with the sacrifices? Why do costume-clad dancers move frenetically in their presence? Why are they the beneficiaries of such devotion?

There is a God-shaped void in the heart of every person. God created us for himself and has placed eternity in our hearts. We long for something, someone bigger than we are. We desire the hole to be filled, but want to fill it on our own terms with things we buy or build. However, only God is the one who can fix the hole in your heart. Destroy your idols and fall on your knees before him.

Father, reveal my idols. Show me the things I bow before. Forgive me for my missed focus. I am on my knees. Lift my head and let me see only you. In Jesus' name. Amen.

NOVEMBER 27

Psalm 136:1-9

Give thanks to the L*ORD*, *for he is good.*
　　His love endures forever.
Give thanks to the God of gods.
　　His love endures forever.
Give thanks to the Lord of lords:
　　His love endures forever.

to him who alone does great wonders,
　　His love endures forever.
who by his understanding made the heavens,
　　His love endures forever.
who spread out the earth upon the waters,
　　His love endures forever.
who made the great lights –
　　His love endures forever.
the sun to govern the day,
　　His love endures forever.
the moon and stars to govern the night;
　　His love endures forever.

His Love Endures Forever

Our heavenly Father is the God of gods and the Lord of lords; and . . . he is good. Everything he does is right. His love is unconditional. He has provided the way to himself through his Son, Jesus. We belong to him because of "his enduring loyal love."

Twenty-six times in this Old Testament song, worshipers repeated, "His love endures forever." It was a deep theological truth that the psalmist did not want people to miss or forget. The repetition engraved this truth deep into the Israelites' minds.

Even when news is not good, God is. Even when the job goes away, God doesn't. Even when we feel alone, we're not. Even when we feel rejected, God wraps us in hands of acceptance. God's love carries us through each day of our lives and then carries us home. Thanksgiving is a daily celebration because God's love endures forever.

Father, thank you for your eternal love and eternal life through Jesus. In his name I pray. Amen.

NOVEMBER 28

Psalm 136:10-16

to him who struck down the firstborn of Egypt
    His love endures forever.
and brought Israel out from among them
    His love endures forever.
with a mighty hand and outstretched arm;
    His love endures forever.
to him who divided the Red Sea asunder
    His love endures forever.
and brought Israel through the midst of it,
    His love endures forever.
but swept Pharaoh and his army into the Red Sea;
    His love endures forever.
to him who led his people through the wilderness;
    His love endures forever.

His Love Endures Forever (continued)

When a person tells me that a particular song has too much repetition, my standard response is: "Have you ever read Psalm 136?" Twenty-six times the psalmist wants us to repeat, "His love endures forever." Twenty-six times we are to proclaim the wonder of God's enduring loyal love. Why?

Someone has well said that we need to be reminded more than we need to be taught. Everybody loves new bits of information, a new nugget of knowledge. Knowledge comes dressed up like spiritual growth, but it is a dreadful imposter. It's the movement of truth twelve inches down from the head to the heart that changes the course of a life.

The psalmist drives home each one of God's actions with the underlying reason. He acts because he loves us. He not only struck down the Egyptians and parted the Red Sea, but God so loved the world that he sent his only Son to die on the cross for your sins and mine. That's a love that should never stop being celebrated.

Father, thank you for your enduring, loyal love. Help me to repeat it continually in my heart, in my head, and with my hands. In Jesus' name. Amen.

NOVEMBER 29

Psalm 136:17-22

to him who struck down great kings,
    His love endures forever.
and killed mighty kings –
    His love endures forever.
Sihon king of the Amorites
    His love endures forever.
and Og king of Bashan –
    His love endures forever.
and gave their land as an inheritance,
    His love endures forever.
an inheritance to his servant Israel.
    His love endures forever.

His Love Endures Forever (continued)

Jerry Bridges describes God's love this way: "God's unfailing love for us is an objective fact affirmed over and over in the Scriptures. It is true whether we believe it or not. Our doubts do not destroy God's love, nor does our faith create it. It originates in the very nature of God, who is love, and it flows to us through our union with His beloved Son."

Psalm 136 is one place in Scripture where the love of God is confirmed over and over. The psalmist reminds the readers of the great works that God has done; great works that he did specifically for them! These actions of God on their behalf are confirmations of his enduring loyal love.

Think back on your life and consider all the things that God has done for you. Start at your beginning; he gave you life itself. Recall the times he has saved you from heading down the wrong path or came to your rescue when you took a detour. Remember when he met you in your loneliness and discouragement. Thank God for his forgiveness, for separating your sins as far as the east is from the west. Bless the Lord for all of his blessings to you. As Bridges says, "Our doubts do not destroy God's love, nor does our faith create it." God's love resides in his Person and, like his Person, his love endures forever.

Father, thank you that your love for me never runs out. Thank you for loving me when I am far from loveable. Thank you that your love for me originates with you and covers me by the work of Jesus on the cross. In his name I pray. Amen.

NOVEMBER 30

Psalm 136:23-26

He remembered us in our low estate
    His love endures forever.
and freed us from our enemies.
    His love endures forever.
He gives food to every creature.
    His love endures forever.

Give thanks to the God of heaven.
    His love endures forever.

His Love Endures Forever (continued)

God will never forget you. Others may, but not God. Friends will come and go, neighbors will move in and out. Sometimes even family members will walk away, but God always has us on his mind. Even when we fall away he will never write us off. He remembers us in our low places, the places where others will leave us be. He stoops down to lift us up.

His love endures forever.

God will never leave us captive. Sin comes in the form of unbreakable chains. The locks are secure. In our best Houdini-like efforts we remain chained, trapped, caught. The Enemy comes to destroy us while we are imprisoned. We are no match for his power or deception. After all, he is a liar and the father of lies. However, God comes to our rescue. He opens the locks and frees us from certain death. He gives us eternal freedom.

His love endures forever.

God gives us everything we need. His presence satisfies our starving souls. His mercy quenches our desperate thirst. His food never runs out and never gets old. He gives us everything we need to do everything he calls us to do. When we come to the end of our lives, we don't have to fear. He will carry us home.

His love endures forever.

Father, I give thanks to you, the God of heaven. I thank you for your eternal covenant of loyal love purchased in full by Jesus. In his name I pray. Amen.

DECEMBER 1

Psalm 137

By the rivers of Babylon we sat and wept
    when we remembered Zion.
There on the poplars
    we hung our harps,
for there our captors asked us for songs,
    our tormentors demanded songs of joy;
    they said, "Sing us one of the songs of Zion!"

How can we sing the songs of the L<small>ORD</small>
    while in a foreign land?
If I forget you, Jerusalem,
    may my right hand forget its skill.
May my tongue cling to the roof of my mouth
    if I do not remember you,
if I do not consider Jerusalem
    my highest joy.

Remember, L<small>ORD</small>, what the Edomites did
    on the day Jerusalem fell.
"Tear it down," they cried,
    "tear it down to its foundations!"
Daughter Babylon, doomed to destruction,
    happy is the one who repays you
    according to what you have done to us.
Happy is the one who seizes your infants
    and dashes them against the rocks.

When I Don't Feel Like Singing

Let's face it, we are not always in a singing mood. There are periods when praise won't come. Prayer is stymied by persistent pain. Thanksgiving is driven away by a chronic circumstance. Sometimes our eyes are filled with tears, our mouths are filled with sobs, and our hearts ache.

After the reign of King Solomon the kingdom of Israel was split by civil war. The Assyrians captured the Northern Kingdom in 722 BC. The Babylonians ransacked the Southern Kingdom in 586 BC. The Israelites were taken captive, prisoners in a foreign land. One day a Babylonian guard demanded, "Sing us one of the songs of Zion!" But Israel didn't feel like singing. Joy is hard to come by when you are far from home. Instead of singing, they "sat and wept."

Today you may be weeping as well. The tears will come, but don't despair. Paul reminds us that when we don't know how to pray the Holy Spirit is praying for us at a depth we cannot even begin to comprehend. He has your back. He is on your side. You may not feel like praying, but he does and he is. Today, God himself is praying for you! Joy will come again.

Lord, like the captive Israelites, today I have hung my harp in the trees and I don't feel like singing. Still I know that you are on my side and will never leave me. Thank you. In Jesus' name. Amen.

DECEMBER 2

Psalm 138:1-5

Of David.

I will praise you, Lord, with all my heart;
    before the "gods" I will sing your praise.
I will bow down toward your holy temple
    and will praise your name
    for your unfailing love and your faithfulness,
for you have so exalted your solemn decree
    that it surpasses your fame.
When I called, you answered me;
    you greatly emboldened me.

May all the kings of the earth praise you, Lord,
    when they hear what you have decreed.
May they sing of the ways of the Lord,
    for the glory of the Lord is great.

Emboldened

The most common Hebrew word translated "glory" was a commercial term that referred to a pair of scales. The word meant, "to be heavy." An item that was substantial on the scales was valuable; it had intrinsic worth. The word came to describe a person's "importance" and "worthiness." As the psalmist says in today's song, "the glory of the Lord is great." There is no one like him.

God's greatness, his "weightiness," his "worthiness," his "glory," is why the psalmist desires to sing praise with all his heart. God's love never fails. He is faithful in all he does. We are "emboldened" to know that the eternal God hears and answers our prayers.

As believers we have the privilege of speaking with the Maker of heaven and earth. We are encouraged to call the God of all glory our Father, even Abba (Daddy). We are invited into the intimacy of one who loves us beyond our ability to grasp and has plans for us beyond our wildest dreams. That's why, with the psalmist, we say, "I will praise you, Lord, with all my heart."

Thank you, Father, for your unfailing love.
Thank you, Father, for your faithfulness.
Thank you, Father, for hearing my prayer.
Thank you, Father, for answering.
Your presence in my life emboldens me.
In Jesus' name. Amen.

DECEMBER 3

Psalm 138:6-8

Of David.

Though the Lord is exalted, he looks kindly on the lowly;
    though lofty, he sees them from afar.
Though I walk in the midst of trouble,
    you preserve my life.
You stretch out your hand against the anger of my foes;
    with your right hand you save me.
The Lord will vindicate me;
    your love, Lord, endures forever –
    do not abandon the works of your hands.

God Stooped Down

God stooped down. Although he is exalted, he looks kindly on the lowly.

God stooped down. Though lofty, he still sees me right where I am.

God stooped down. He is there in my challenges.

God stooped down. He saved my life.

God stooped down. He protects me from my enemies.

God stooped down. He defends me.

God stooped down. His love never quits on me.

God stooped down. He will never abandon me.

God stooped down to breathe life into Adam.

God stooped down to breathe eternal life into my dead soul through Jesus.

The amazing truth of Scripture:

God stooped down.

Thank you, Father, for loving me in my lowly state.

Thank you, Lord Jesus, for taking on flesh and dying for my sins.

Thank you, Holy Spirit, for daily empowerment.

Thank you for stooping down.

In Jesus' name. Amen.

DECEMBER 4

Psalm 139:1-6

For the director of music.
Of David. A psalm.

You have searched me, Lord,
    and you know me.
You know when I sit and when I rise;
    you perceive my thoughts from afar.
You discern my going out and my lying down;
    you are familiar with all my ways.
Before a word is on my tongue
    you, Lord, know it completely.
You hem me in behind and before,
    and you lay your hand upon me.
Such knowledge is too wonderful for me,
    too lofty for me to attain.

Looking for a Hiding Place?

Have you ever tried to hide from God? Sometimes it's tempting, isn't it? We try to find a dark place where no one can see our actions. We snuggle up in an emotional corner to stroke our secrets. We head for a mental open range where our thoughts can run free. However, we can never hide from God.

In the opening verses of Psalm 139, David proclaims God's omniscience. He knows everything there is to know about everything there is to know. Whether I am sitting still or on the move, whether I am far from home or in my bed, God is "familiar with all my ways." My words never take him by surprise. I can't escape the One who surrounds me on all sides.

How should I respond to God's all-knowing nature? The person of God is "too wonderful for me," "too lofty for me to attain." He knows me inside and out. He has my back. He will never let me out of his sight. I will never be out of his mind. He will carry me all the way to eternity. I can respond to such a Person only in humble worship. There is no need to hide from God.

Father, today is the day that I stop trying to hide from you. I stand open, bare and vulnerable. Search me and show me my sin. Help me to repent. I worship you alone. In Jesus' name. Amen.

DECEMBER 5

Psalm 139:7-12

For the director of music.
Of David. A psalm.

Where can I go from your Spirit?
> Where can I flee from your presence?
If I go up to the heavens, you are there;
> if I make my bed in the depths, you are there.
If I rise on the wings of the dawn,
> if I settle on the far side of the sea,
even there your hand will guide me,
> your right hand will hold me fast.
If I say, "Surely the darkness will hide me
> and the light become night around me,"
even the darkness will not be dark to you;
> the night will shine like the day,
> for darkness is as light to you.

God Is Omnipresent

God is not limited by time or space. He is present everywhere at the same time in his whole being. There is nowhere in the entire universe, on land or sea, in heaven or hell, that a person can go and get away from God.

Admittedly, there are times when this is a disturbing truth. In our rebellion we want to escape God's presence. We don't want him around when we engage in sinful activities, but God doesn't play hide and seek. Wherever we go, he is already there.

Most of the time that truth is comforting. Because of God's omnipresence we are never alone. He is there in our laughter and our tears. He is there when we pump our fists with excitement and when we hang our heads in despair. He stands by our side as we watch our loved ones breathe their last. He walks with us from the grave and through our grief. He never leaves us nor forsakes us. The omnipresent God is Immanuel – God with us – through eternity.

Father, forgive me when I try to get away from you. Thank you for never leaving my side. In Jesus' name. Amen.

DECEMBER 6

Psalm 139:13-18

For the director of music.
Of David. A psalm.

For you created my inmost being;
> you knit me together in my mother's womb.

I praise you because I am fearfully and wonderfully made;
> your works are wonderful,
> I know that full well.

My frame was not hidden from you
> when I was made in the secret place,
> when I was woven together in the depths of the earth.

Your eyes saw my unformed body;
> all the days ordained for me were written in your book
> before one of them came to be.

How precious to me are your thoughts, God!
> How vast is the sum of them!

Were I to count them,
> they would outnumber the grains of sand –
> when I awake, I am still with you.

Does Your Life Matter?

Have you ever wondered if your life really matters? In quiet moments do you contemplate what kind of impact you are making? In those reflecting minutes before falling asleep do you ever question your significance and value? Well, I can assure you that God is not thinking those thoughts about you.

God has always had you on his mind. Before your first moment of life he knew all about you. He watched you grow in your mother's womb. Like Michelangelo's "David" and da Vinci's "Mona Lisa," you are God's masterpiece and more priceless than any painting. In fact, before you came to be he had charted all the days of your life. You were created to do the good works that God prepared in advance for you to do (Ephesians 2:10). He sent his Son to die just for you and is preparing your eternal home. One day he will take you there to live with him forever.

Does your life matter!? Every second of your every day matters to God!

Father, thank you for life. Thank you for the complex systems that make up my body. Thank you for an earth that allows me to live and breathe. Thank you for Jesus, who allows me to know you. Thank you for your Holy Spirit, who empowers me. Thank you for your generous and gracious gift of life! In Jesus' name. Amen.

DECEMBER 7

Psalm 139:19-22

For the director of music.
Of David. A psalm.

If only you, God, would slay the wicked!
    Away from me, you who are bloodthirsty!
They speak of you with evil intent;
    your adversaries misuse your name.
Do I not hate those who hate you, Lord,
    and abhor those who are in rebellion against you?
I have nothing but hatred for them;
    I count them my enemies.

Responding to the Wicked

Religious extremists behead innocent people and video their evil acts for the world to see. Christians are herded like animals, marched to the edge of town and executed. Believers around the world are persecuted because they refuse to renounce their faith. Wicked, bloodthirsty people desire to destroy everyone and everything associated with God. How are we to respond?

David had such passion for God that he could not stay quiet about his feelings toward the wicked. He saw God's enemies as his enemies. He knew they were intent on damaging the kingdom. His hatred was a boiling, righteous indignation as a result of seeing God being dishonored.

When Jesus saw the worship of God being turned into a moneymaking scheme, he made a whip of cords and drove the culprits from the temple. The disciples remembered the words of David, "zeal for your house consumes me, and the insults of those who insult you fall on me" (Psalm 69:9). David could not stand by emotionless as God was being insulted. Neither should we.

Father, stir my indignation for the things that oppose you. Help me to respond with love and conviction, gentleness and passion. Don't let me be silent when others insult you. In Jesus' name. Amen.

DECEMBER 8

Psalm 139:23-24

For the director of music.
Of David. A psalm.

Search me, God, and know my heart;
    test me and know my anxious thoughts.
See if there is any offensive way in me,
    and lead me in the way everlasting.

Searchlight on My Heart

In a time of personal reflection, the prophet Jeremiah wrote, "The heart is deceitful above all things and beyond cure. Who can understand it?" (Jeremiah 17:9). Left on my own there isn't much I can't rationalize. My sin can be excused as something I deserve. Whoever believes his heart is not deceitful is deceived! That's why today's passage should be our daily prayer.

David concludes this powerful psalm with an invitation for God to shine a searchlight on his heart. He calls God to reveal anything hidden. He desires testing to see where anxiety pushes away faith. He asks God to point out the sin so he can seek forgiveness.

I am the absolute worst judge of my motives. I need outside counsel to assess my state. I need the Counselor to lay open my heart and search every part I am trying to hide.

Father, I ask you to shine your searchlight on my heart. Make known my heart. Show me where I am missing the mark. Make known my anxious thoughts so I can turn them from worry to trust. Show me where I am offensive to you and others. Please don't let me live my life doing things that offend others by my personality, actions or words and not even know the damage I'm causing. Please don't let me live in an offensive way to you and never seek your forgiveness. Father, help me follow hard after you as you lead me home. In Christ's name. Amen.

DECEMBER 9

Psalm 140:1-5

For the director of music.
A psalm of David.

Rescue me, Lord, from evildoers;
   protect me from the violent,
who devise evil plans in their hearts
   and stir up war every day.
They make their tongues as sharp as a serpent's;
   the poison of vipers is on their lips.

Keep me safe, Lord, from the hands of the wicked;
   protect me from the violent,
   who devise ways to trip my feet.
The arrogant have hidden a snare for me;
   they have spread out the cords of their net
   and have set traps for me along my path.

Dealing With Enemies

Do you have any enemies? Any person who would like to see you slip and fall? A person who talks behind your back? Maybe a few people who try their best to actually cause you to fall?

David had a few enemies. There were foes that devised evil plans and tried to drag David and his men into war. Adversaries slandered him with sharp tongues, "the poison of vipers is on their lips." Some set traps for David to succumb. His nemeses wouldn't stop until they saw David go down.

David knew that he was no match for the evil plans, poison rumors and hidden traps, so he turned to God for help. He prayed that God would rescue him and protect him "from the violent." He asked God to keep him safe and guard him from the hidden traps. David's prayer can be yours as well . . . if you have any enemies.

Father, I am no match for my enemies. They are shrewd. They are persistent. I am afraid that I will let down my guard and fall. Please protect me. Please rescue me. Please keep me safe. Please guard me against my enemies. In Jesus' name. Amen.

DECEMBER 10

Psalm 140:6-13

For the director of music.
A psalm of David.

I say to the L<small>ORD</small>, "You are my God."
*   Hear, L<small>ORD</small>, my cry for mercy.*
Sovereign L<small>ORD</small>, my strong deliverer,
*   you shield my head in the day of battle.*
Do not grant the wicked their desires, L<small>ORD</small>;
*   do not let their plans succeed.*

Those who surround me proudly rear their heads;
*   may the mischief of their lips engulf them.*
May burning coals fall on them;
*   may they be thrown into the fire,*
*   into miry pits, never to rise.*
May slanderers not be established in the land;
*   may disaster hunt down the violent.*

I know that the L<small>ORD</small> secures justice for the poor
*   and upholds the cause of the needy.*
Surely the righteous will praise your name,
*   and the upright will live in your presence.*

The Day of the Battle

Every day is a day of battle for the believer. The Enemy is suited for war. He is looking for a weakness, an opening. He waits to find an unguarded moment. He stalks for a time to pounce and devour. He is shameless. He waits . . . for fatigue, discouragement, pride. There are no rules by which he plays.

David prayed for the day of battle. He prayed that God would show mercy and be his "strong deliverer." He asked God to be the shield on his head. He knew the enemy was ruthless and would hold nothing back. He knew his only hope of deliverance was with God.

Every day is a day of battle for the believer. Like David we proclaim to the Lord, "You are my God." Our hope is not in our strength or intelligence. We know that left to ourselves defeat will come. Our prayer is David's prayer. Lord, show your mercy. Lord, be my strong deliverer. Lord, shield my head in the day of battle. Lord, let me live in the peace of your presence.

Father, hear my prayer. I depend on you and you alone. I am no match for my enemies. Be my strong deliverer. In Jesus' name. Amen.

DECEMBER 11

Psalm 141:1-4

A psalm of David.

I call to you, Lord, come quickly to me;
    hear me when I call to you.
May my prayer be set before you like incense;
    may the lifting up of my hands
    be like the evening sacrifice.

Set a guard over my mouth, Lord;
    keep watch over the door of my lips.
Do not let my heart be drawn to what is evil
    so that I take part in wicked deeds
along with those who are evildoers;
    do not let me eat their delicacies.

Reckless Words

Reckless words pierce like a sword (Proverbs 12:18). The emotional weapon forms in our hearts and the blade shoots from our lips. There are times we enjoy watching the pain. Our words are premeditated and purposeful. There are also times when we wish with every ounce of our being that there was a way to delete every syllable that poured from our lips.

David knew the danger of reckless words. That's why he prayed, "Set a guard over my mouth, Lord; keep watch over the door of my lips." David knew his weakness, his propensity. He needed God to stand like a soldier guarding the camp, like a watchman on a wall.

This should be our daily prayer: O Lord, guard my words! Keep watch over my lips! Shut my mouth. Help me think before I speak. Don't let those I love go through life with the wounds of my reckless words.

Father, David's prayer is mine – Set a guard over my mouth, Lord; keep watch over the door of my lips. Do not let my heart be drawn to what is evil. In Jesus' name. Amen.

DECEMBER 12

Psalm 141:5-10

A psalm of David.

Let a righteous man strike me – that is a kindness;
> let him rebuke me – that is oil on my head.

My head will not refuse it,
> for my prayer will still be against the deeds of evildoers.

Their rulers will be thrown down from the cliffs,
> and the wicked will learn that my words
> were well spoken.

They will say, "As one plows and breaks up the earth,
> so our bones have been scattered
> at the mouth of the grave."

But my eyes are fixed on you, Sovereign LORD;
> in you I take refuge – do not give me over to death.

Keep me safe from the traps set by evildoers,
> from the snares they have laid for me.

Let the wicked fall into their own nets,
> while I pass by in safety.

Confrontation Is Kindness

Why do believers let other believers act like unbelievers? Why do followers of Jesus refrain from telling other followers of Jesus that they are not acting like followers of Jesus? Why are some Christians more apt to gossip about other Christians than they are to confront them about their sin?

In today's psalm David invites what Scripture teaches – as iron sharpens iron, so one believer sharpens another. David uses hyperbole to make the point: Confrontation is kindness. It is like refreshing oil being poured over a weary head. If a person is courageous enough to get involved when you step out of line, you know that they really care for you.

Is there a person you need to have a conversation with? A person who seems to be skating on thin ice, spiritually speaking? A person you love too much to let alone? Remember, confrontation is kindness. If the person you confront doesn't thank you today, he or she will tomorrow.

Father, give us the courage to sharpen each other. Give us the courage to guard each other's back. Give us the strength to be kind enough to confront. In Jesus' name. Amen.

DECEMBER 13

Psalm 142

**A maskil of David.
When he was in the cave. A prayer.**

I cry aloud to the Lord;
    I lift up my voice to the Lord for mercy.
I pour out before him my complaint;
    before him I tell my trouble.

When my spirit grows faint within me,
    it is you who watch over my way.
In the path where I walk
    people have hidden a snare for me.
Look and see, there is no one at my right hand;
    no one is concerned for me.
I have no refuge;
    no one cares for my life.

I cry to you, Lord;
    I say, "You are my refuge,
    my portion in the land of the living."

Listen to my cry,
    for I am in desperate need;
rescue me from those who pursue me,
    for they are too strong for me.
Set me free from my prison,
    that I may praise your name.
Then the righteous will gather about me
    because of your goodness to me.

Alone. Afraid. Desperate.

David was on the run and the enemy was closing in. He felt alone "no one cares for my life." His situation was urgent "I am in desperate need." The opposition was too strong for him. Death was certain unless God intervened. David cried for God's mercy. He prayed to be set "free from my prison." David was sitting alone, afraid and desperate in a cave.

Some of you can relate all too well. An illness, a job loss, a relationship heartbreak, abandonment, grief – a significant life situation has imprisoned you. You sense the enemy pursuing you and closing in fast. Like David you are sitting alone, afraid and desperate in your personal cave.

And . . . like David you can "cry aloud to the Lord." Ask God for his mercy. Pour out your complaint before him. Tell him your trouble. He cares for you when no one seems concerned. He is your refuge when there is no place of protection. He is your defender when you are helpless. He is your strength when the enemy is too strong. He is your freedom when you are alone, afraid and desperate in your personal cave.

Father, my prayer is David's. You are my refuge, my portion in the land of the living. Listen to my cry, for I am in desperate need; rescue me from those who pursue me, for they are too strong for me. Set me free from my prison, that I may praise your name. In Jesus' name. Amen.

DECEMBER 14

Psalm 143:1-6

A psalm of David.

Lord, hear my prayer,
    listen to my cry for mercy;
in your faithfulness and righteousness
    come to my relief.
Do not bring your servant into judgment,
    for no one living is righteous before you.
The enemy pursues me,
    he crushes me to the ground;
he makes me dwell in the darkness
    like those long dead.
So my spirit grows faint within me;
    my heart within me is dismayed.
I remember the days of long ago;
    I meditate on all your works
    and consider what your hands have done.
I spread out my hands to you;
    I thirst for you like a parched land.

Desperate!

Where do you turn when your spirit grows faint within you? Where can you find peace when your heart is filled with turmoil? Where can you hide from the enemy who is crushing you to the ground?

David had many challenges throughout his life. For over a decade he ran from a jealous King Saul who was determined to kill him. He spent many days and nights hiding in caves and crying out to the Lord. Often his cries were desperate. His longing for God's deliverance was like a man dying of thirst in the desert.

Maybe your cries are desperate today. You are disappointed with your current situation. Discouragement has settled over your heart like a dense fog. You long for God; and . . . he longs for you. He hears your cry for mercy. He is coming to provide relief. Hold on! The heavenly Father will always take care of his children, now and forever.

Father, hurry to my rescue. I am not sure how much longer I can hold on. Bring light to my darkness and hope to my helplessness. Quench my thirst with the comfort and confidence of your Spirit. In Jesus' name. Amen.

DECEMBER 15

Psalm 143:7-12

A psalm of David.

Answer me quickly, Lord;
> my spirit fails.
Do not hide your face from me
> or I will be like those who go down to the pit.
Let the morning bring me word of your unfailing love,
> for I have put my trust in you.
Show me the way I should go,
> for to you I entrust my life.
Rescue me from my enemies, Lord,
> for I hide myself in you.
Teach me to do your will,
> for you are my God;
may your good Spirit
> lead me on level ground.

For your name's sake, Lord, preserve my life;
> in your righteousness, bring me out of trouble.
In your unfailing love, silence my enemies;
> destroy all my foes,
> for I am your servant.

Deliver Me Safely Home

In this portion of Psalm 143 David prays for four things. Let's make David's requests our own.

Lord, let the morning bring your unfailing love. Unfailing love is the translation of "hesed", a rich Hebrew word that describes a love of covenant, a love that will never let us go. Let God know how much you desire this love that holds you close and never releases you.

Lord, rescue me from my enemies. Ask God to protect you from those who would want to see you fall or who are trying to make you fall. Ask him to protect you from the Enemy who constantly seeks your destruction.

Lord, teach me by your Spirit. Ask God to show you the path to take and the decisions to make today. Ask him to teach you to do his will. Ask him to give you the desire and the focus to follow hard after him.

Lord, preserve me. Ask God to protect you, to keep you safe. Ask him to keep you walking close to him. Ask him to continue the good work that he started in you. Ask him to deliver you safely home.

In Jesus' name. Amen.

DECEMBER 16

Psalm 144:1-4

Of David.

Praise be to the L<small>ORD</small> my Rock,
*   who trains my hands for war,*
*   my fingers for battle.*
He is my loving God and my fortress,
*   my stronghold and my deliverer,*
my shield, in whom I take refuge,
*   who subdues peoples under me.*

L<small>ORD</small>, what are human beings that you care for them,
*   mere mortals that you think of them?*
They are like a breath;
*   their days are like a fleeting shadow.*

Covered!

Praise be to the Lord . . .

. . . My Rock: He is the One I run to for refuge. With him I can never be moved.

. . . My Fortress: He is the One I stand behind for protection. Behind his walls I am defended.

. . . My Stronghold: He is the place where I hide from my enemy. In him the enemy will never find me.

. . . My Deliverer: He is the One who snatches me from the jaws of defeat. The enemy is powerful, but no match for my deliverer.

. . . My Shield: He is the One who always has my back. His shield guards me on all sides.

Father, thank you for being my Rock, my Fortress, my Stronghold, my Deliverer, my Shield. My hope and trust is in you alone. In Jesus' name. Amen.

DECEMBER 17

Psalm 144:5-11

Of David.

Part your heavens, Lord, and come down;
> touch the mountains, so that they smoke.

Send forth lightning and scatter the enemy;
> shoot your arrows and rout them.

Reach down your hand from on high;
> deliver me and rescue me

from the mighty waters,
> from the hands of foreigners

whose mouths are full of lies,
> whose right hands are deceitful.

I will sing a new song to you, my God;
> on the ten-stringed lyre I will make music to you,

to the One who gives victory to kings,
> who delivers his servant David.

From the deadly sword deliver me;
> rescue me from the hands of foreigners

whose mouths are full of lies,
> whose right hands are deceitful.

Fresh. New. Bold.

It's time to get out of the rut. It's time to stop singing the same old song, praying the same worn out prayer, falling into the same ugly sin. Yesterday is in the past. Its challenges are over – won some, lost some. Today is a new day. It is time to sing a new song.

David was a songwriter and well prepared to make music to God. With his ten-stringed lyre he composed beautiful songs to the One who gives victory and delivers his servants. God rescued David from nature, warriors, and even those "whose mouths are full of lies." From the heat of the desert to the mouth of the deceitful, God always comes through.

Are you ready for a new song? Ready for something fresh, new and bold? Get out of the rut. Listen to new music. Read a fresh portion of Scripture. Visit with a person in a nursing home. Share the Gospel with a friend. Go someplace where you can sing at the top of your lungs. Get out of your rut. Sing a new song.

Father, forgive me for being stuck. Help me get unstuck. Put a new song in my heart that is fresh and bold. Let me sing it like I have never sung it before. Stretch me to worship you with renewed joy. In Jesus' name. Amen.

DECEMBER 18

Psalm 144:12-15

Of David.

Then our sons in their youth
>*will be like well-nurtured plants,*
and our daughters will be like pillars
>*carved to adorn a palace.*
Our barns will be filled
>*with every kind of provision.*
Our sheep will increase by thousands,
>*by tens of thousands in our fields;*
>*our oxen will draw heavy loads.*
There will be no breaching of walls,
>*no going into captivity,*
>*no cry of distress in our streets.*
Blessed is the people of whom this is true;
>*blessed is the people whose God is the LORD.*

God's Dynamic Work

God's work is evident to all. Sometimes he stretches you with challenges. Sometimes he brings great blessing and joy. Sometimes his work causes you to sing a new, fresh and bold song. God's work in your life is dynamic, never static.

David noted that the people whose God is the Lord are blessed. Their young men are spiritually rooted like well-nurtured plants. Their daughters stand strong like pillars carved to adorn a palace. God fills their barns with food and their pastures with livestock. God's work results in great blessings.

God is at work all around you. He delivers plenty of food. He puts a roof over your head. He gives meaningful work for sustenance and generous giving. God is at work in your life. Open your eyes! Don't miss his blessings.

Father, help me to see you at work in my life. Make me aware of your actions and help me respond with heartfelt thanksgiving. In Jesus' name. Amen.

DECEMBER 19

Psalm 145:1-7

A psalm of praise. Of David.

I will exalt you, my God the King;
    I will praise your name for ever and ever.
Every day I will praise you
    and extol your name for ever and ever.

Great is the Lord and most worthy of praise;
    his greatness no one can fathom.
One generation commends your works to another;
    they tell of your mighty acts.
They speak of the glorious splendor of your majesty –
    and I will meditate on your wonderful works.
They tell of the power of your awesome works –
    and I will proclaim your great deeds.
They celebrate your abundant goodness
    and joyfully sing of your righteousness.

Experience God's Goodness

The story of God is settled in Scripture, and he uses people to pass it on. One generation tells the story of God's greatness to another. We tell the stories of the Bible and share the experiences of God's good work in our lives. God gives us a story to tell! Then we pass it on with passion.

How do you experience the mighty acts of God so that you can pass them on with passion? Here are a few ideas.

- **Share the Gospel with a friend or family member.** You will never get over the joy of leading a person to Christ.

- **Serve at a local mission or shelter.** While you are serving find some time to hear the story of those in the mission or shelter. When you take the time to serve, God works in your heart in powerful ways.

- **Serve in your local church.** Every believer has at least one gift. Use it to serve others.

- **Go on a short-term mission trip.** Away from your personal comfort zone you see God at work in new and exciting ways. Every mission trip I take I see God in refreshing ways and am personally stretched.

Father, I want to share impassioned stories with my children. Help me combine the truth of your Word with the passion of real life experiences. Give me stories to tell of the times when you were powerfully at work in my life. In Jesus' name. Amen.

DECEMBER 20

Psalm 145:8-13

A psalm of praise. Of David.

The Lord is gracious and compassionate,
> slow to anger and rich in love.

The Lord is good to all;
> he has compassion on all he has made.

All your works praise you, Lord;
> your faithful people extol you.

They tell of the glory of your kingdom
> and speak of your might,

so that all people may know of your mighty acts
> and the glorious splendor of your kingdom.

Your kingdom is an everlasting kingdom,
> and your dominion endures through all generations.

The Lord is trustworthy in all he promises
> and faithful in all he does.

Paid in Full

God is gracious! He gives us what we don't deserve and could never earn. His gift of salvation was purchased in full by Jesus on the cross and is offered to all. The gift is presented free of charge without condition.

God is compassionate! He saw our need and did something about it. He sent his Son to pay the penalty of sin. In compassion God stooped down to do for us what we could not do for ourselves. He cleanses our hearts and gives us a fresh start.

God is slow to anger! God does not treat us as our sins deserve. He is patient with our human failure and stubbornness. He welcomes us home when we leave for a time and do regrettable things. He wishes that none perish but all would repent and come home.

God is rich in love! God loved the world in this way: He sent his Son to die on our behalf on the cross. Jesus came to bear our sins in his body at Calvary. He took the wrath of sin for us.

Lord Jesus, how can I ever begin to thank you for your great love? Words cannot express my gratitude. Help me thank you with my life. In your name. Amen.

DECEMBER 21

Psalm 145:14-21

A psalm of praise. Of David.

The Lord upholds all who fall
    and lifts up all who are bowed down.
The eyes of all look to you,
    and you give them their food at the proper time.
You open your hand
    and satisfy the desires of every living thing.

The Lord is righteous in all his ways
    and faithful in all he does.
The Lord is near to all who call on him,
    to all who call on him in truth.
He fulfills the desires of those who fear him;
    he hears their cry and saves them.
The Lord watches over all who love him,
    but all the wicked he will destroy.

My mouth will speak in praise of the Lord.
    Let every creature praise his holy name
    for ever and ever.

The Lord Upholds

The journey is filled with dangers. The road signs for temptations are brightly lit, attractive and luring. The path has a treacherous downhill grade and some exhausting climbs. Sometimes we get worn down. Sometimes we fall down.

> *But the Lord upholds all who fall and lifts up all who are bowed down.*

The journey is filled with decisions. There are different paths to different destinations. Our assessments are not always wise, our judgments not always prudent. Sometimes our choices weigh heavily on our souls.

> *But the Lord upholds all who fall and lifts up all who are bowed down.*

The journey is filled with dreams. There are things we want to accomplish. There are aspirations we long to achieve. The path does not always arrive at the doorstep of our desires. The death of our dreams leads to the land of great disappointment.

> *But the Lord upholds all who fall and lifts up all who are bowed down.*

Lord, thank you for holding me up even when I take the wrong path, make the wrong decision and follow the wrong dream. Thank you for holding me up every step of the journey and delivering me home in victory! In Jesus' name. Amen.

DECEMBER 22

Psalm 146:1-5

Praise the Lord.

Praise the Lord, my soul.

I will praise the Lord all my life;
 I will sing praise to my God as long as I live.
Do not put your trust in princes,
 in human beings, who cannot save.
When their spirit departs, they return to the ground;
 on that very day their plans come to nothing.
Blessed are those whose help is the God of Jacob,
 whose hope is in the Lord their God.

Confidence

What delivers confidence? What brings calmness? What produces peace? What gives you hope? A thriving economy? A stable job? Your person in the White House? A hefty retirement account? A strong military?

Check out today's passage. Human beings – even the most powerful – cannot save. Even the most impressive person will die, robbing them of any semblance of power. On the very day the big shot dies, his hubris dies with him.

Who are you going to trust? Where are you turning for confidence? If your hope is not found in the Lord, sooner or later your teetering tower of trust will come crashing down. Without God it's just a matter of time before your faux calm turns to feverish chaos; but there is One who is eternal. He remains faithful forever. Blessed is the one whose confidence is in him.

Father, it is tempting to put my trust in the stuff and people around me. Give me great leaders, but never let me forget that you are the only One who will stand for eternity. Help me follow hard after you. In Jesus' name. Amen.

DECEMBER 23

Psalm 146:6-10

He is the Maker of heaven and earth,
    the sea, and everything in them –
    he remains faithful forever.
He upholds the cause of the oppressed
    and gives food to the hungry.
The Lord sets prisoners free,
    the Lord gives sight to the blind,
the Lord lifts up those who are bowed down,
    the Lord loves the righteous.
The Lord watches over the foreigner
    and sustains the fatherless and the widow,
    but he frustrates the ways of the wicked.

The Lord reigns forever,
    your God, O Zion, for all generations.

Praise the Lord.

Faithful Forever

This passage is loaded with the activities of God. Check these out.

He remains faithful forever.
He will never renegotiate a promise.
He fights for the oppressed.
God lifts up those who are beaten down.
He gives food to the hungry.
He takes care of his own.
He sets the prisoners free.
The chains of sin were broken at the cross.
He gives sight to the blind.
Those living in darkness have seen a great light.
He lifts those who are bowed down.
He offloads heavy burdens.
He loves the righteous.
His love extends all the way to the cross.
He helps the helpless.
He helps those who can't help themselves.
He frustrates the wicked.
He wins every time.
He reigns forever.
He is the eternal King!

Father, you are the Maker of heaven and earth. Thank you for your constant work in my life today and throughout eternity. In Jesus' name. Amen.

DECEMBER 24

Psalm 147:1-6

Praise the Lord.

How good it is to sing praises to our God,
 how pleasant and fitting to praise him!

The Lord builds up Jerusalem;
 he gathers the exiles of Israel.
He heals the brokenhearted
 and binds up their wounds.
He determines the number of the stars
 and calls them each by name.
Great is our Lord and mighty in power;
 his understanding has no limit.
The Lord sustains the humble
 but casts the wicked to the ground.

The Holy Healer

God stands by the brokenhearted, but he doesn't just stand by. He is not a passive onlooker. He comes to us in our brokenness as the Divine Doctor, the Sovereign Surgeon. He is the Holy Healer. He brings exactly what we need at the precise moment we need it; not a moment too soon, not a second too late.

God stands by the brokenhearted. He comes to broken bodies and broken dreams. He arrives at the right time with the right prescription and injects us with the healing power of his Spirit. When he brings healing, confusion is driven away by calmness; panic is chased off by peace. He finds all the places where doubt has broken through and rebuilds the wall.

God stands by the brokenhearted. Difficult times can leave us in painful places. We feel like God has left us and let us down. The "Why?" question is never far from our minds. Spiritual and physical exhaustion wear us down. God comes to bind up our wounds. Don't hide your hurt. Uncover your wounds so he can gently bind them with his tender touch.

Heavenly Father, thank you for standing by me in my brokenness. Thank you for binding my wounds. Help me uncover any wound I may be hiding. Thank you for your powerful work in my life. In Jesus' name. Amen.

DECEMBER 25

Psalm 147:7-14

Sing to the L<small>ORD</small> with grateful praise;
    make music to our God on the harp.

He covers the sky with clouds;
    he supplies the earth with rain
    and makes grass grow on the hills.
He provides food for the cattle
    and for the young ravens when they call.

His pleasure is not in the strength of the horse,
    nor his delight in the legs of the warrior;
the L<small>ORD</small> delights in those who fear him,
    who put their hope in his unfailing love.

Extol the L<small>ORD</small>, Jerusalem;
    praise your God, Zion.

He strengthens the bars of your gates
    and blesses your people within you.
He grants peace to your borders
    and satisfies you with the finest of wheat.

God With Hands

God sent his Son not as a conquering warrior, but as a baby. He took away every privilege of deity in order to demonstrate his unfailing love to man.

Tiny hands waving about uncontrollably. A shrill cry piercing the damp air of a borrowed cave. A peaceful smile on the lips of a mother wearied by labor. A mysterious smile on the face of the mother's husband who has helped deliver a miracle. **The Incarnation: God confined to an infant.**

Growing hands pointing to the ancient scrolls. An adolescent voice asking and answering questions. The teachers of the Law, amazed at His understanding. A mother who "treasured all these things in her heart." The Father smiling with favor. **The Incarnation: God growing in stature.**

Powerful hands turning water into wine, feeding multitudes, touching life into lifeless bodies. Thankful faces without words to express their gratitude. A mother's smile as she hears of her Son's marvelous deeds. **The Incarnation: The Father being glorified through the Son.**

Bound hands led away by Roman soldiers. Tied in complete submission to the eternal Plan. A mother waits; the dreaded time has come. The Father controls the final blow to sin. **The Incarnation: "Like a lamb led to slaughter . . . He did not open His mouth."**

Constricted hands; the result of spikes driven through His wrists. Arms outstretched; nailed to a wooden beam. A mother looks on, feeling every painful throb as her own. The just Father turns His back on His burdened Son. **The Incarnation: ". . . the Lord caused the sin of us all to fall on Him."**

Scarred hands in resurrected glory. A chariot of clouds lifting Him to the Father. A joyful mother watching her Son ascend. A promise from the lips of the risen Savior: Just as I go, I will return again. **The Incarnation: The assurance of our resurrection.**

Open hands inviting every sinner. Accepting all who come to Him in faith. Blind eyes see; prison doors are opened. The prince or pauper; none are turned away. Eternal life for all who trust the Son. **The Incarnation: Sinful man in communion with the eternal Father through His Son.**

Merry Christmas!

DECEMBER 26

Psalm 147:15-20

He sends his command to the earth;
   his word runs swiftly.
He spreads the snow like wool
   and scatters the frost like ashes.
He hurls down his hail like pebbles.
   Who can withstand his icy blast?
He sends his word and melts them;
   he stirs up his breezes, and the waters flow.

He has revealed his word to Jacob,
   his laws and decrees to Israel.
He has done this for no other nation;
   they do not know his laws.

Praise the Lord.

The Heart Melter

It is an absolute fact of spiritual growth: You cannot grow unless you are regularly reading God's Word. His Word is a lamp to our feet and light to our path. It points us to the right path, tells us when we stray, shows us how to get back on the path, and challenges us to stay on the path of obedience. God's Word judges the thoughts and intentions of the heart.

In the day this psalm was written fast runners carried messages. The psalmist likens God's Word to one of those message carriers. God's Word "runs swiftly." The Lord personally delivers it to those who follow him, just in time. When we receive the message it "melts" us and stirs our passions. God's Word produces action in our lives.

Now is the time to make commitments for a new year. My challenge to you is to commit to reading God's Word every day. Scripture is our spiritual food. It nourishes our hearts and quenches our thirst. God desires to melt your heart, stir your passions, and encourage you for action. This coming year make it your resolution to read God's Word.

Father, thank you for your Word that melts, challenges and encourages my heart. Help me make the commitment to read your Word each day. Give me the encouragement to follow through with that commitment. In Jesus' name. Amen.

DECEMBER 27

Psalm 148:1-6

Praise the Lord.

Praise the Lord from the heavens;
    praise him in the heights above.
Praise him, all his angels;
    praise him, all his heavenly hosts.
Praise him, sun and moon;
    praise him, all you shining stars.
Praise him, you highest heavens
    and you waters above the skies.

Let them praise the name of the Lord,
    for at his command they were created,
and he established them for ever and ever –
    he issued a decree that will never pass away.

Call to Praise

The psalmist sounds the call for all God's people. It is a call to praise. Let's take time today to answer the call and praise the Lord. I encourage you to use this guide each day to proclaim your worship to the living God.

Praise God for causing you to see your sin and need for a Savior.
Praise God for introducing you to Jesus and allowing you to trust him.
Praise God for giving you his Holy Spirit to comfort, convict and empower you.
Praise God for his Word that melts, impassions and encourages your heart.
Praise God for the church where you find spiritual connection.
Praise God for the spiritual growth that he is allowing in your life.
Praise God for health.
Praise God for the physical challenges that he is using to grow you.
Praise God for your mother and father.
Praise God for your godly boyfriend/girlfriend.
Praise God for your husband/wife.
Praise God for the gift of children.
Praise God for friends who love, encourage and spur you on.
Praise God for the job he has provided.
Praise God for the roof over your head.
Praise God for the daily provision of food.
Praise God for his great creation – sun, moon and shining stars.
Praise God for another day of life.
Praise God for his mercies that are new each morning.
Praise God for the home that awaits you in heaven.
Praise the Lord!

Father, you alone are worthy of all my praise. Help me proclaim your greatness throughout each day of my life. In Jesus' name. Amen.

DECEMBER 28

Psalm 148:7-14

Praise the L<small>ORD</small> from the earth,
> *you great sea creatures and all ocean depths,*

lightning and hail, snow and clouds,
> *stormy winds that do his bidding,*

you mountains and all hills,
> *fruit trees and all cedars,*

wild animals and all cattle,
> *small creatures and flying birds,*

kings of the earth and all nations,
> *you princes and all rulers on earth,*

young men and women,
> *old men and children.*

Let them praise the name of the L<small>ORD</small>,
> *for his name alone is exalted;*
> *his splendor is above the earth and the heavens.*

And he has raised up for his people a horn,
> *the praise of all his faithful servants,*
> *of Israel, the people close to his heart.*

Praise the L<small>ORD</small>.

Praise Prompter

Need a reason to praise the Lord? This passage gives several praise prompters.

- When you see the great creatures of the sea on the National Geographic channel . . . Praise the Lord!
- When you stand on the beach and look out over the vast ocean . . . Praise the Lord!
- When lightning cracks across the sky . . . Praise the Lord!
- When hail pounds the earth . . . Praise the Lord!
- When each unique snowflake falls from the clouds . . . Praise the Lord!
- When the storm clouds roll . . . Praise the Lord!
- When you view a grove of fruit trees and a forest of cedars . . . Praise the Lord!
- When you observe wild animals with their amazing instincts . . . Praise the Lord!
- When you drive by a pasture filled with cattle . . . Praise the Lord!
- When you watch small creatures in their habitat . . . Praise the Lord!
- When you look up to see a bird soaring in the sky . . . Praise the Lord!

Kings and princes, young and old, men and women . . . all are called to praise the absolute magnificence of the God who is above all things. Look around you! God is at work – God is always at work. Praise the Lord!

Father, don't let me miss one opportunity to praise you. Help me to open my eyes and see your magnificence and power all around me. In Jesus' name. Amen.

DECEMBER 29

Psalm 149:1-5

Praise the LORD.

Sing to the LORD a new song,
> *his praise in the assembly of his faithful people.*

Let Israel rejoice in their Maker;
> *let the people of Zion be glad in their King.*

Let them praise his name with dancing
> *and make music to him with timbrel and harp.*

For the LORD takes delight in his people;
> *he crowns the humble with victory.*

Let his faithful people rejoice in this honor
> *and sing for joy on their beds.*

The Eternal King

Praise is not mumbled with eyes cast down; it is shouted with eyes raised up. Praise does not get bored with worn out lyrics that lose their meaning with conditioned repetition. Honoring God should be fresh and new. Rejoice in your Maker, the eternal King.

Praise does not normally radiate from a hands-in-pockets stance; it involves bodily expression. Maybe it's with an uplifted hand, or even two. Maybe it's with some movement to demonstrate that you're alive. For sure praise is accompanied by music – even loud music – with percussion and strings and horns. Rejoice in your Maker, the eternal King.

Praise is founded on a theological truth: God takes delight in YOU! He loves you so much that he sent his Son to pay the penalty for your sin. When you humble yourself before him, he personally places a crown of victory on your head. When you know that God is on your side, you can go to bed still singing songs. You can rejoice in your Maker, the eternal King.

Father, help me praise you with everything I have! Help me to get just as excited about you as I do my favorite sports team. Help me rejoice in you through all things. You are my Maker, my eternal King. In Jesus' name. Amen.

DECEMBER 30

Psalm 149:6-9

May the praise of God be in their mouths
    and a double-edged sword in their hands,
to inflict vengeance on the nations
    and punishment on the peoples,
to bind their kings with fetters,
    their nobles with shackles of iron,
to carry out the sentence written against them –
    this is the glory of all his faithful people.

Praise the L ORD .

Get a Grip

In the Old Testament the nation of Israel served as God's instrument to execute judgment on her enemies. The warriors fought for God's honor with his praise in their mouths and a double-edged sword in their hands. They battled with the Lord's power and for his honor.

Like Israel, believers today are in a battle. Our struggle is not against flesh and blood, "but against the rulers, against the authorities, against the powers of this dark world and against the spiritual forces of evil in the heavenly realms" (Ephesians 6:12). To prepare for battle we need protective gear, the full armor of God. The only offensive weapon in our cache is "the sword of the Spirit, which is the word of God" (Ephesians 6:17). The writer to the Hebrews says that God's Word is alive and active, "sharper than any double-edged sword." It penetrates the soul, judging the "thoughts and attitudes of the heart" (Hebrews 4:12).

Believers must go into each day's battle with a tight grip on Scripture, our double-edged sword. We must read, study and meditate on God's Word. We must memorize it and hide it securely in our hearts. We must be those who live out the truth. No warrior would think about going into battle without the proper gear. The same goes for the believer. May the praise of God be in our mouths and the sword of the Spirit in our hands.

Father, give me the desire to be in your Word. Prepare me for each day's battle. Equip me with the sword of the Spirit. In Jesus' name. Amen.

DECEMBER 31

Psalm 150

Praise the L*ord*.

Praise God in his sanctuary;
praise him in his mighty heavens.
Praise him for his acts of power;
praise him for his surpassing greatness.
Praise him with the sounding of the trumpet,
praise him with the harp and lyre,
praise him with timbrel and dancing,
praise him with the strings and pipe,
praise him with the clash of cymbals,
praise him with resounding cymbals.

Let everything that has breath praise the L*ord*.

Praise the L*ord*.

The Great Hallelujah

The final psalm is the great hallelujah (the Hebrew word for "Praise the Lord"). It begins and ends with this one-word proclamation of admiration and honor. In between the two hallelujahs are exhortations to praise God at all places, in all times, with all we have.

Let's close this year with "Praise the Lord" on our lips. Praise him for his work in your life over the past months. Praise him for "his surpassing greatness." Praise him for "his acts of power." Tell him that you would have never made it through this year without him by your side.

Begin a new year praising God with your lips and with your life. Let everyone know that you serve the King of Kings and the Lord of Lords. Demonstrate to all those in your world that you will honor him with obedience, that you will stand for him even if you have to stand alone. Praise the Lord – loud and long!

Father, you alone are worthy of all my praise. I praise you for this year and I praise you for a new year. May my life be a song of praise proclaiming my love for you, the King of Kings and the Lord of Lords. In Jesus' name. Amen.